The Neverending Love of God

Loving Light Books

Book One - God Spoke through Me to Tell You to Speak to Him
Book Two - No One Will Listen to God
Book Three - You are God
Book Four - The Sun and Beyond
Book Five - The Neverending Love of God
Book Six - The Survival of Love
Book Seven - We All Go Together
Book Eight - God's Imagination
Book Nine - Forever God
Book Ten - See the Light
Book Eleven - Your Life as God
Book Twelve - God Lives
Book Thirteen - The Realization of Creation
Book Fourteen - Illumination
Book Fifteen - I Touched God
Book Sixteen - I and God are One
Book Seventeen - We All Walk Together
Book Eighteen - Love Conquers All
Book Nineteen - Come to the Light of Love
Book Twenty - The Grace is Ours

Loving Light

Book 5

The Neverending Love of God

Liane Rich

The information contained in this book is not intended as a substitute for professional medical advice. Neither the publisher nor the author is engaged in rendering professional advice to the reader. The remedies and suggestions in this book should not be taken, or construed, as standard medical diagnosis, prescription or treatment. For any medical issue or illness consult a qualified physician.

Loving Light Books
Original Copyright © 1990
Copyright © 2009 Liane

All rights reserved. This book may not be copied or reproduced in any form whatsoever, without written permission from the publisher, except for brief passages for review purposes.

ISBN 13: 978-1-878480-05-7
ISBN 10: 1-878480-05-7

Loving Light Books
www.lovinglightbooks.com

for Rosie

The information in this series is not necessarily meant to be taken literally. It is meant to *shift* your consciousness...

Forward

Anyone immersed in the vast body of new metaphysical knowledge is aware of the virtual symphony of voices from channeled sources throughout the world - inspirational voices that may be artistic, poetic, philosophical, religious, or scientific. And now, out of these myriad New Age voices, comes a series of books by God, channeled through Liane, revealing the frank truth in all its glory and wonder, telling us how to cleanse our bodies, gain access to our subconscious minds, clear our other selves and march back to who we are - God.

In God's books you will be introduced to a loving, powerful, gripping, exciting, and often humorous voice that reaches out and speaks ever so personally to the individual reader. As the reader's interest deepens, invariably an intimate relationship to this voice develops. It is a relationship that lasts forever, and I am quite certain I do mean forever.

Here is an accelerated program, a no-holds-barred course, where God guides us and loves us, and as needs be recommends books to us and even a movie or musical piece along the way. He (She) enters our lives and sees through our eyes, seeming to enjoy the ride as He guides us back to US, back to ALL. Here is a voice that is playful and informative, that is humorous and serious, that is gentle and powerfully divine. It is a voice that knows no barriers or restrictions, a straightforward and honest voice that caresses us when we need the warmth and pushes us when we are immobilized.

In today's New Age literature there is an avalanche of information from magnificent beings of light, information that possesses us and compels us to look at our fears and express our love. In this series of books by God, you will find truly powerful methods for making this transition from toxicity to purity, from density to light, from fear to love, and from the delusion of death to the awakening to full life. You will experience in these books the love and the power of God for it is your love to express and your power to behold. Rarely will you see more lucid steps for transformation. Read these beautiful words and rejoice in our period of awakening, our return to Home.

John Farrell, PhD., LCSW. - Psychologist, Clinical Social Worker, Senior Clinician Psychiatric Emergency Services, U.C. Davis Medical Center, Sacramento. John is also a retired Professor - California State University, Sacramento, in Health Sciences and Psychology.

The Neverending Love of God

Introduction

God, are you light? Yes, now I will write for our new book...

Once upon a time I did not wish to be the only source of this solar system and so I began to split and send out more of me to fill in where I thought energy was needed. Now that I "see" how this energy has been used I am unhappy and even a little sad that this is what I chose.

So how can God who is all knowing and all things not *know* how to be God and create as God? I will explain. God is not all knowing any longer. God got so confused by mixed emotion and mixed reaction to those emotions that now God is split in his decision as to what is or is not about to occur. You see, God is light, however God is also light vibration and God does not wish to be anything else until you become light also. The only problem with this entire theory is that only light has the ability to "see" clearly, and since God is growing and expanding as *everything* I am becoming everything, and since you are more debris or darkness than light I am now becoming what you are, as you project all back to me. So how does God on high clear and become light once again? I must clean my body and clear my cells of debris and darkness, and in clearing I will allow me to be light or God force once again. And who or what are my cells? Right... *they are you.*

You are the cells in the body of God and I wish you to clear to allow God to clear darkness and debris. You are not to be so concerned with clearing your neighbor's problems as with your own problems. You begin to clear by cleaning up your own mess and then cleaning up your mother (earth) and then cleaning up your air and then cleaning up your solar system. Then *you* will be light and that one cell in God's body that is you will be vibrating at such a speed that it's light vibration affects all other cells, and now we have one "clear" cell who is literally affecting millions of others just by "being" light. In the same way that one bad apple can spoil the entire barrel of apples; one good cell can effectively "activate" the entire body of cells. And once activated these cells begin to rise up and create a powerful light system that is capable of moving planets and stars and even your sun.

So now you know and I wish you to clear you. Start at home when you begin to worry about this planet and its problems and even the animals and their problems. All begins and ends with you. You do not force another to bathe and you do not force another to change and you do not force another to love. Love is God and when God is clear we *will* have love, not war, and peace on earth. This is a promise that I will keep to you, the children of the planet. You will see peace on earth and of course peace will bring happiness. Clean up your messes and clean out your bodies and all will be well. God does not wish to be left out of you and your plans. Please ask God to return as you have pushed me out of your bodies and I am not allowed anywhere uninvited. Invite God back into your lives and you will be inviting "light" back into you.

You are not so unloving as you pretend to be. You are love at its best and you are God at his best. We must clean you up so that you shine and then we will clear you and you will be God once again. No big loud protest movement. Just simple change and simple techniques and simple thoughts. These are God's ways. No big complicated plan. God works in simple ways and God teaches simplicity. No complication - only openness and un-complication. This is your key to kindness and love and happiness at this time.

Love and live and think and eat simply. Do not complicate your life with specialty items. Un-complicate and unravel and un-prepare. You are all "prepared" for the worst and so of course you receive what you prepare for. It is not necessary to fear life to such a degree as to create war and violence and even mass hysteria over being robbed and being murdered and being unloved. You are at the panic stage in your development on this planet, and now you are running to and fro, and your thoughts are scattered and you are attacking at every turn. And each time that you attack or lash out at another you are attacking or lashing out at a neighbor cell in God's body. God does not wish for his body to be at war within itself. Allow all attack thoughts to pass and all love thoughts to prevail.

Now I will leave you with this thought. You are not the only living energy force on this planet and you are not "in" control so stop pretending to be. Allow this planet to clear and allow your body to clear. You will not be allowed to commit suicide any longer. Stop killing you with hate thoughts and stop killing your neighbor with guns. You are now at a turning point on this planet. You may continue with the old ways and be left outside of God or you may walk to the light and *change*. You make this choice as all choice is yours. No pushing, no threatening. Either you are with God or you stay. No big deal. Stay as you are and allow confusion to reign and to rule over you or walk into God's light and allow confusion to fade as the light goes on. You must decide. I do not force you nor do I judge you in this choice.

I will now end this, the introduction to my fifth book in this "Loving Light" series. You now may look to yourself for your way out of your confusion. I do not wish to interfere; however I am confident that you will see the benefits involved. You do not learn to live in love by creating chaos and screaming how wrong everyone else is. You learn to live in love by being clear and balanced and this is what you will learn in this book. *"The Neverending Love of God"* is just that - love that is eternal. I am the "I am" - the source that began it all. There is no end and in actuality there is no beginning. There only is, right now, right here, this moment in time. I love you and I do not wish to convince you to clear. I wish you to want to clear and to come home to the light.

God

Once you began to get the idea that you are not so bad you left behind judgment. Now you are learning to clear and release and shine. I don't want to be a nuisance here, however it is important to teach you to heal *you*. You are no longer the person who first began to read God's books. You have triggered release and cleared these thoughts from the subconscious and now your subconscious is not so full of debris and trapped negative thought. Thought is energy and in clearing these thoughts you are clearing how you *now* think. The old thought patterns govern this present you and convince this present you that you are at the end of your "good" on earth. These old thoughts have taught you to *fear* in place of *love* and now you are coming back to God and learning to love and not fear.

You have spent a great deal of time judging your every move and now I wish you to stop judgment of you; as in judging you, you are judging me. I am God and I projected into you and now I am working through you and you spend so much time talking about how rotten life is treating you and how bad people are, and now you have the opportunity to go beyond yourself and accept. Accept *all* that occurs and allow it to be. No wrong way. No right way. Just the simplest of all... "being." Allow all to be exactly what all is - no use of scare tactics, no use of protection *against* another and no use of firing at one another. You fire the moment someone does not agree or fit into your idea of what is best for you. Allow all to be exactly who and what they are as this will allow you to be exactly as you are.

This is *important*. Do not change or save others. They are here to learn to save themselves. Do not get so involved in their lesson that you take their learning from them. Walk your own path and act and look and discover your own way. You do not get back to God by pushing and shoving at the rest of the world. You get back to God by pushing and practicing what you preach. Do your own homework. Work on you till there is no more to work out and you will no longer draw any discomfort to you. You will see only peace and calm and love with no "bad stuff," as you call it.

So, this is your lesson for today. Do not criticize what is happening in your world because you do not know the big plan and just maybe what you look at with horror is actually very, very good. You don't know what is happening on other levels and you don't know how "action" creates effect, and you don't know which of those on earth are more your energy and therefore more of you.

So, stop criticizing because criticism creates fear and your world is now so full of fear that I cannot get into you. You walk and talk how advanced you are and you are so full of fear that God cannot speak to you or write through you. You are not so tough as you believe. You are still in your infancy and you fear what you do not understand. This girl has not once stopped her writing. She has experienced setbacks but she does not give up. Others believe she is crazy for what she does but she does not give up. She has given up all because a big voice once spoke to her and asked her to write God's books. So simple - I work so simply and you will not believe. She has been my instrument now for over two years.

Oh, yes, I know, you are each and everyone an instrument of God. So why is it that you don't hear my voice and why is it that you don't allow me to write to you and why is it that you don't move to my request and why is it that I do not have the ability to speak freely to you on a daily basis? Free Will! Your gift of free will keeps God out of your life. I do not mean spiritually. Many of you walk with God and talk *to* God.

How can I convince you to become clear and allow me to actually communicate as we once did? At one time I could speak with each of you and add to your lives. Now I am a prisoner in my own self. I am not allowed to talk because God is too busy to speak to people. "God doesn't waste his time writing books for us. Why would he? He's doing bigger and more important things. He's saving the world and talking to our guardian angels and telling them what to say to us because he's royalty and royalty does not mix with the peasants." And so I sit and cannot get through to you.

God is *in* each of you, which makes you part of God and yet you will not allow God to speak to you because you believe you do not deserve to hear from God, or in some cases you simply "fear" God so much that you do not wish to come face to face with him. You have taught and been taught that I judge you as being good or evil and so you do not wish to face me and hear my verdict! I do not judge you ever. Only you judge you. I only ask to be allowed to help you.

Can you imagine how all this looks for me? I sit here and write to my own cells to explain how things are and my own cells won't listen. How do I get you to listen? You all seem to know best. You all seem to have your own view of this information and how it is being channeled. You do not give this information the power it deserves because you are so busy trying not to be tricked. You won't be fooled. You won't be duped. You won't even be thankful for this information, because it may not be God and God forbid if you should begin to listen to someone or something that is not the one and only God.

So, how can I convince you that I am who I say I am? Liane even has her doubts at times. There is so much disbelief at God writing books that she wonders if she is wrong in her belief that I am God. She doesn't really care at this point since she has cleared sufficiently to just go with the flow of her life. She creates very little stress over anything and she seems to just "know" the right direction or answer for her. This is no accident of course. You see; she has been prepared - prepared by me to write my books. And yes, it took some work and determination on her part but she knows she was being moved by something much larger than herself.

All this was done as she asked. Yes, she asked to be put in her right place and she repeatedly asked that I take over her life for her. She trusts *God*. Most of you fear God to the point of panic at the mention of my name. "How dare she use the name of God like this? How dare she use God's name on these books? She is not channeling God; she is channeling her own higher self or personality. We know, because God would not bother with one channeler." And, of course, you all have your own version of these statements.

So, how do I convince you that I am God? I do not. Believe it, or not! We don't care. Liane and I simply do not care. She has come to a place where it is not necessary to sell this information or convince you to talk with God. God does not care if you believe or not. Not enough to take away your free will and the gifts of trust and faith anyway. So; you and Liane are just the same. She has her doubts and you have your doubts. And that's okay too, because you are now working out of faith and if you continue to read, it is out of faith and trust in this information. And if she continues to write it is out of trust and faith.

So, go out and tell anyone who is ready to hear, that God does take the time to write for his children. Each of you is important in every way that matters because each of you make up God's body. I will now leave you with this thought, "do not judge those who do not believe this information, as you will be judging God who is you..."

※

You do not wish to believe *in* me so I will now tell you another story. Once upon a time I began to contemplate my own self and I began to see how I was becoming and growing and expanding, and now I have taken a good look at what I have become and I wish to change. I wish to become love and light once again. I do not wish to be the only source of darkness in that I do not wish to be taken over by darkness. My light has begun to dim simply because this dark energy is growing and light vibration is dimming to the point of extinction. Look around you. You and your world are the body and God. Do you see light or do you see darkness? Do you see love or do you see fear? Do you run and sing and dance and love out of joy or do you run and hide out of fear. When you play is it because it feels good or is it out of an urgency and searching for joy?

You no longer live by instinct. Your instinct will tell you that you are attracted to someone and you hear from another that this someone may have a reputation for suffering and harming others and so you do not allow you to get involved with this someone who is being drawn to you. You stand back and watch as others get involved with this person and they come away and say, "Oh boy did I get hurt by this one." And you pat yourself on the back and congratulate yourself because you did not take a chance and get hurt.

Then lo and behold you see this special someone who has this reputation for breaking hearts and he or she is with one person and in love and happy and they do very well together and become an item. And now you wonder what was wrong with you. Why didn't you win the heart of this special heart breaker and now I will explain. You do not wish to go out on a limb. You wish to play it safe. You wish to be in security and not in love. You do not wish to give love... you wish only to receive then you may think about giving. You will play the part and act the part but when it comes time to reach out and hold love in your hands you will run and hide because you believe you do not deserve love. So, you will say "I love you" and act "I love you" as long as he or she is showing love. When he or she begins to stop "demonstrating" love you stop extending and showing love.

This is not unconditional. This is love that is set on the condition that you return another's love only if it feels good and comfortable. And when these conditions are not met, you then lose your love for one another and you walk away and you believe that this relationship was just not good for you, and you move on to the next and so on and so forth. And here we find you today and you are all searching for love and you find it and you say, "No, this is not what I want," and I will now tell you the problem.

You are a gold miner who does not know gold when he sees it. How can you dig up a treasure if you do not know what the treasure looks like? You are searching for and finding love and the first sign of a problem you throw down your pick and shovel and move on to a new dig. This is not what God had in mind when he came into human form. This was not meant to be so taxing and trying. This was experimenting and playing with clay. We were building and sculpting and creating and now you have created a clay form for yourselves and you are trapped within this form and cannot get out. You are so afraid of love that you refuse to call one another out of fear of sounding foolish to those you truly care about. How can expressing love be foolish? How can saying, "I love you no matter what," be stupid? How can you *not* spread my words of love in such an over darkened world?

And each and every time that you "express" and "show" love it returns and hits you right where you live... in love with you. Your "I love you" expressed to another, comes right back at you and is "I love you" expressed to you. You are the only one here. There is no other. God has but one body and that body that is God is everyone and everything and when you show love for another you are simply showing love for you. One cell in God's body "showing" love to another cell adds to the entire body. If you can learn to go into your fears and show love, regardless how foolish you believe yourself to appear, you will raise the vibratory level of the entire body of God.

Whatever choices you make affect the whole. If you choose to hide in your fear and wait for another to show love first, you will add fear to the entire body. You may add light to the whole by being what you are which is love essence and love vibration. The natural you, who is spirit and essence, wishes to love and you, out of your fear, wish to suppress this love so you will not be hurt or maimed in this battlefield of love. You have chosen to create war on this planet and now you are choosing to fight love. You wish to stop love from expressing and this will not be allowed. *I will not allow love to die.*

Hear me on this subject because I do not wish to repeat myself. I am God and I am telling you to *love*. Love yourself and love your neighbor and love those whom I send to you at this time. You are killing love by fearing love and this will not be permitted. I will expect to see each of you reaching out instead of turning your back on love. You do not see how foolish you truly are. You spend a fortune on books and tapes and dating services and when I send you a partner you shout, "Oh no, this is not what I ordered." How can you possibly know what is best for you when you do not even know who you really are?

───※───

You do not believe you are in a position to be of help to God at this time. You spend your time running and hiding and you do not trust *you* to do the right thing. I will now explain how you will save this planet! You will begin to raise your light vibration to the extent that you will create added light. This added light will affect all who are part of this solar system and beyond.

Now, in our first three books we explained how all on earth are actually part of earth, and even how all on earth are part of the same energy source and therefore part of the whole. All are connected and even interwoven. So now we have you all woven together and you are dirty. This big blanket that is God is dirty and is in need of cleaning and so I will now begin to launder out the dirt and grime and even the stains. No more debris to soil God. We begin with one of you and begin to clear. And one of you literally spreads the soap and water as you soak it up, and this will continue until the entire blanket that is God is soaked with soap and water. And we begin to agitate and we see the soil go out in the rinse water and the blanket becomes shiny clean. The soap and water is awareness and the agitation is enema. And you who began with me in Book One, *God Spoke through Me to Tell You to Speak to Him*, know how this works.

So, if you have not yet read our first three books, I suggest you close this, our fifth book, and go out and purchase Book One. No one will be able to understand this information without first reading books one through four. This is important. I do not wish to frighten any *away* from this material and this is exactly what will occur if you are not prepared. So, close this book and do not open it until your subconscious mind has been properly prepared. I do not ask that you do this, I only suggest, as I know you and how obstinate you can be when you wish to do it your way.

So, I suggest you take a good look at how clear your life is and how secure and happy you are before you move on into this advanced information. I guarantee that you will not only lose your sense of interest in this book, you will also create further confusion for your conscious self. Much of the information given is directed to other you's on other levels of reality and reading this material without preparing your conscious mind is very unkind to "self." So, be good to your self and allow self to "see" gradually how all really is. You will enjoy this progress.

Now, for those who are my fifth graders, welcome back and happy reading. I will see you all in class tomorrow for more informative reading and I do hope you have been practicing your lessons.

So now I have you wondering once again what to do when you are in love with the "wrong" person. Let me tell you first of all that there is no wrong person for you. You will draw to you exactly what you are and exactly what you wish to learn to overcome. In some cases, what you are is very difficult for you to see. We all believe that we know best and when you believe that you have the right answers, it is difficult to show you how rightness is not always goodness. Thus, the ego, who is rightness, jumps up and says, "No, this situation will not do. I must leave this situation with this person." So now you have ego shouting at you to leave and you have fear of how big this unwanted situation with this person may become and so you leave. You do not wish to ride out the storm and go through the cleanup after the storm, so you pack yourself up and you leave and do not wait to consider that this person may not be wrong for you after all. You abandon ship!

Now, how do you know who is right for you at this time? If you find him or her attractive or intriguing in some way and you are somehow drawn to them, then you are likely "drawing them to you." So, stop running from what you draw. You are seeing "you" in them. Often you will not see you clearly and you will wish to know that I will show you how to do this. You do not look at him or her and say, "Oh no, this can't be me. I never do this or that." This is not how images work. They will sound or act a certain way and you will see that they are nervous or over reacting or shy or strangely quiet or even loud and you will know that this is you, hating the part of you that is nervous or shy or strangely quiet. And when you begin to see how this is you, you will begin to see how you too are them and they have been drawn to show you who you are.

Now, when you "receive" one who has big psychological problems or even big physical handicaps, you are dealing with a part of you that is buried and is not expressing properly. This may be as simple as a part of you that does not know how to love or a part of you that does not know how to express as love. These gifts are very powerful and will enlighten you immensely. When you draw a "biggie" to you, you grow in leaps and bounds. Some of you on earth at this time are moving quite rapidly and are drawing the big ones. There are two things that I wish you to remember when dealing with relationships on this planet. Number one: this is a good time to look into your mirror and discover who you really are, and number two: when you love another out of spiritual love you do not find fault with them *ever*. You find only love and you receive only love.

So, know that if you are finding fault with your lover it is you who is out of balance and not your loved one. You have drawn this to you to show you how you are acting and re-acting, and often times this is on another level and is not consciously you. You will wish to know that all are in this together and the partner I have sent you is also working on his or her lessons. And you each agreed in another time to become student and teacher. So, thank your teacher for loving you enough to show you "you" and hug them and kiss them and know that they are you.

Go to your teacher and look at your own image and when you have seen "you" in them, you will no longer be out of balance.

You do not wish to be in love, as you believe that to be in love is to own. You do not own one another as you are not the owner of your system. Most of you feel that when you are in love you create a boundary and lay floor plans and develop the land and it becomes yours. You put down your own problems and begin to work on your lover's problems and insist on "fixing" everything that is not right with them. So far none of you are perfect unless you "accept" all as perfect. So who is to say that the one you love is not perfect just the way he or she is and it is only in your eyes that they lack perfection? Many of you are praying for the perfect mate or the right mate and I will tell you now that the one I send is perfect for you and you will learn most about you from this one who you believe needs to change.

Now, when you receive a mate who does not fit your needs, I suggest that you look again. You will find that this mate is not only a gift; he or she is actually going to be good for you in your search for you. I will explain. Say you have received a mate who does not conform to your expectations of what is or is not acceptable. I highly suggest you begin to look at why you chose to draw this mate to you. It could be as simple as taking a look at how you once did not conform to your own expectations. So, how do you love one who does not conform? You allow them to be exactly who they are and go on your merry way and do not enforce your rules on them. When you go you simply say, "I love you and I want you but not at this price." You do not insist that they change nor do you ask them to change. You bring this situation back to you because it begins with you. If you want someone to stop smoking or drinking or fighting or being stubborn, you must not change them you must change you.

So, this does not sit well with you and I will explain. When you love someone who does not wish to change and you are not happy with them as they are you are compromising you for them. Do not compromise. Be you by allowing them to be them. Love them as they are and allow them to "see" clearly that you love them and then either accept them as they are or negotiate and find a solution. And if a solution does not come, allow them to be and give them your love and allow you to be by being you without compromise. Do not override the will of another by being what they do not or cannot accept. In other words, you are killing you by forcing you to accept a situation that is not compatible or good for you.

You will wish to know that in shrieking at, or pushing at the one you love to change, you are expecting to own he or she - and no one is permitted to own another. You may "accept" and love without condition but to own is prohibited as all are already part of God and no one owns God. So, love them and allow them to see this love for them and show them how you love you by not allowing you to be in a position that is not good for you. You will wish to know that you too are in need of love and comfort and to put yourself and your feelings last is to deny that you are God, just as is your mate or friend. Do not short change you by being left out of your own love. Do not give up on you as you are God and they are God and they have volunteered to show you who you are. And in doing so you learn and grow and they learn and grow.

I hope this will allow you to express "I love you" freely. Most of you believe "I love you" to mean "I am committed to you no matter what," and this is simply not so. You may love and not accept, and you may love and not like, and you may even love and want out. And in some cases to love is to share and in some cases to share is to have common goals. And once in a great while, to love is simply to give love to see how love will grow. Love does not begin and end with your command. Love does not go on like a light. Love is and was and will never end and when you fall in love you simply tap into the source that is always there. Do not expect so much of this thing you call love. It is not new. It always was and you began to fear it and now you do not know how to use it properly and this is what I will show you in this, *The Neverending Love of God*.

You do not write love letters as you once did. At one time in your history you wrote to communicate and your letters were filled with love and openness and you saw in your own words how you really felt. To express on paper is very good for you and to express love on paper will show you how you truly love. Do not be so shy about writing "I love you." You will find it gratifying to both you and your loved one. I do not wish to bore you with my own love letters but I will assist each of you if you will simply ask. I love you and I will assist you in this love relationship. For those who are alone at this time I will assist you in loving you and soon we will draw a good mate and you too will be confused by love and asking me, "Why God, why did I get this one?"

It seems that you do not appreciate my gifts and I must teach you to love the one who is actually best for you at this time. Love all who come and you will be loving all parts of you. You are not certain who you are and this is a good time to see clearly by looking into your own mirror. You are the "A" Team. You are my first group and I do not wish you to be in confusion nor out of love with self. All is teaching you to love you. There is a difference between loving and accepting you, and hiding from your fears. You will not accept some, as they show you what you fear. Do not move out of a relationship because you fear what is taking place. Move only out of love.

If it is not good and right for you do not force you to stay. No wrong, remember? We have established that there are no victims. You all volunteer. So, pack your victimization and put it where it belongs - beside love for this teacher. If he or she "abuses" it is to show you what *you* asked to see in order to learn to overcome. You do not shout at your diving instructor when he pushes you out of the plane at 10,000 feet. He is only doing what you requested. You wished to learn to sky dive and now that your teacher is pushing you out, you scream abuse. No abuse occurs. You ask for and receive. So, I suggest you take a good look at this relationship and see how you are teaching you and even what you are teaching you.

You have been off balance for so long that to bring you back into balance is a big job. You have not done what you have wanted to out of guilt that you would do wrong, or fear that you would be rejected. Most of you do not love one another; you simply stay out of loyalty, or fear of what is out there for you if you choose to leave your mate. No one on earth at this time is in true spiritual love. Those of you, who do love and understand that you are with your right mate and in your right place, do not wish to love unconditionally. You have your rules and he or she must understand you or you go crazy. Why is it that you must think alike in order to love one another? Why can't you carry your own belief system and still love one another?

You have fought through the ages to have unity and conformity and this is silly. Allow each different color to be. Each color has a purpose and you are melding all into one big rainbow that is not very bright, as all the colors in your rainbow are being taught to "be" how others "be." Do not use one another to practice your control. Let go and let God and let the other Gods be. Do not convince others to be who you are and do not convince others to be like you and do not convince any to look to you for their answers. Allow all to be exactly who they are and allow you to love them exactly as they are and one day you just may discover *unconditional love*.

So, how do you love someone who thinks and acts and believes different? You act and think and believe for you and soon you will each be respecting one another for being and not pretending. And this respect will grow and become love. And love will conquer all fears of inadequacy and love will teach you to accept without controlling. And soon all on earth will be controlling only themselves and no one will be *expected* to perform to another's tune. *You do not know how to love.* And I am here to teach you that love is you and you are love and you have forgotten and you no longer love, you only think you do.

So, do not be so hard on your neighbor for not being capable of "keeping" his wife or her husband. That is exactly what you are doing on earth. You are "keepers" not lovers. And you control whoever you keep and you make certain that they dance to your tune or you leave and do not return just to punish them. And they know that you are the boss and so they submit so as to learn because if they do not learn you will not love them. Love them as they are and they will grow in your love and they will not be owned by you any longer. They will simply be loved. And to love is to support and to support is to share. And to share is to be you and share you with them and allow them to share with you. And soon we will have all this loving and sharing and no one will be left out. And no one will be hurt or confused as to how he or she should act because he or she will be happy and accepted just as they are.

I do not wish to continue to harp on this subject of unconditional love, so I will simply say that to love *you* without restriction is best. When you begin to love yourself and allow yourself to be who you are without judging yourself as lazy or worthless or unpredictable, you will be allowing you to be. And this will come as a great relief to you... the spirit that is you. You see, you all judge you and you all interfere in the 'right use of will' by commanding you to be better or more worthwhile or more productive or just more acceptable. This is the bottom line. Acceptable means loveable and loveable means worthy of love. And how can you not be worthy of love when you *are* love.

What you see as you is not you. What you see is what you manifested out of your fear of doing wrong and since no one ever is wrong, what you see is simply an illusion. You are not so unlovable nor are you hateful nor are you judgmental. You are simply love and when you accept all of you and stop "seeing" this or that as wrong with you, you will begin to see love... the true essence that is you. You will not find love in your dictionary and you will not find love in a seminar and you will not find love in a lover. You will begin to see love only by accepting you and the reason you become addicted to seminars and self-help groups and lovers is because they tell you that you are okay and even *worth* loving. How can you not be worth loving when you are God?

God does not wish you to continue to draw lessons to teach you how to be good or be better. Stop drawing mirrors that show what is wrong with you and begin to draw mirrors that show you what is right with you. Do not look for the negative in you; look only for the "good" in you and you will see that good in all. You are so careful to not judge yourself for being wise and kind and giving, so why judge yourself for being unkind or stupid or selfish? It makes no sense to judge some characteristics and not others. Judgment kills and destroys and to destroy you is to destroy one of God's cells, and God does not wish his cells to punish nor destroy themselves. So, how do you learn to *accept* you just as you are? You say to yourself "I love you and I accept you" and then you go to sleep. This is a good time to reprogram your subconscious. When you sleep you believe what you are told and so to tell yourself to accept, right before you doze off each night, will have a profound effect on you.

Now I wish to discuss gays. You have been dealing from guilt and pointing a finger at yourself for long enough. Stop it! This is all for now. Know that I accept you just as you are and you too must accept you to become a productive cell once again.

Now, as I have stated previously I am not the only God force on this planet... you are God force also and you and I must join and become whole. I do not require that you do anything other than love. To love is to accept and to accept is to become "all." And to become all is to know all and go home once again. You will not learn to accept by cowering when you are shouted at and you will not learn to accept by arguing back what a good person you are. You learn to accept by knowing that you are good, and when you truly know how good you are you will not feel the need to prove yourself right or to debate or even to defend you. You will sit quietly and simply "know;" and it will not affect you what others believe or do not believe about you.

You who are getting to this stage of your development, will wish to know that you do not have far to go from here. When you can honestly be you without regard for your own insecurities of what others may or may not think, you are ready for my advanced class. Know that enema will assist you in accepting you. With enema, mind control is not so necessary because you begin to "clear" this energy that is judgment and your body let's it go in enema and your "true colors" begin to shine all by themselves. And, oh, do I love to watch you when you are clear and bright. You literally light this universe and fireworks take place for God. You will each come to this place and when you do you will know that judgment is leaving and acceptance is filling its place.

So, don't give up because you are doing a good job being you and soon all will be accepting and loving, and rejection will become a word that once meant something - but no one will remember exactly what. I love you and I accept you as me...

God does not wish to be left out of you and your life. How can I be God and not be interested in what you do? From love to hate, from fear to strength, from envy to sharing - God must become you and is you, so why would God not wish to discuss all aspects of you? You dress so God dresses. You eat so God eats. You harm others so God harms others and you harm you. So God is in a situation that is not so good. God harms himself and now God has become aware and enlightened and is not ready to let you continue. You find it so extraordinary that I would discuss enema and books and your love life and your sex life. I do not wish to explain myself in detail here, however, I will tell you now that what you do or do not do directly affects the whole and *I am that whole.*

So, I ask you to stop harming God and begin to wake up and stop judging God, and begin to love and read and do enema to clear, so that you are strong enough to overcome your past programming. This is so simple. Why can't you believe that God would be concerned? Why would you think that God would *not* be concerned? Don't you realize the extent of yourself and the love that I have for you? How can *you* sit in judgment of me? I am God almighty and you believe that I am some scientific phenomenon and that whatever is channeling through this woman is quite interesting but certainly not God... not the God we know. He wouldn't speak so freely and he wouldn't put things so simply and he definitely would not tell us to read and do enema. So, how do you think I feel when I say who I am and you say, "No you're not? Prove it to us if you are." And soon you will each have your own proof in various ways. For now I will simply say that I do not expect you to believe because you are so confused.

So, how does God on high get the attention of his fingers and toes in order to awaken and save them? This is my job now and I am actually enjoying it. I have seen many begin to stir and a few wake up and even one or two actually stand and shout "I am God and I am going to enema for God." Other than those who do not enema for God there are others who enema out of "awareness" that something good is happening for them and they experience less pain and discomfort and they feel better.

Now, I wish to discuss my Pen. She has a problem yet with writing about enema. She believes God would not push this topic and wishes me to stick to the good information. Oh, she knows enema saved her life and she knows she is now free of illness in her life. She just doesn't want to be the one to sell others on enema. She does not wish to peddle my words as if they are her own and often she does not agree with what I write.

So how is it that she allows me to write what I wish? She is possessed by God. God took over possession of this body at her invitation and she has not requested that I return possession to her. Why? She "feels" better than ever and she senses that she is on a great adventure that is just beginning and she does not wish to be outside of love. She has felt *unloved* for enough of her life and to now feel so much love for life and others is not something she is ready to throw away. She does not at this time know exactly how she does this work, or even why, but she loves love and continues to grow in love with each new day. And the reason she grows in love is that each day she does her enema and clears debris which creates confusion, and the less confusion, the less pain and discomfort. *It's all very simple.* The more light that you carry the less confusion reigns in your life.

Let go of darkness and you become light. Darkness is energy and energy leaves in the water of enema. And you confuse this and create great trauma around this simple little technique. What if you were afraid to brush your teeth or rinse your mouth? You would grow bacteria and begin to smell foul and your gums would begin to decay and your teeth would be weak and food would be considered contaminated before it entered your intestinal tract. How would you solve that mess? You would simply clean out your mouth. Decay would eventually end and your teeth would begin to shine and soon the gums would be strong again and your food would not decay even before it hit the stomach.

Clean out your bowels. You have never cleared the excess debris and it grows daily and it is compounded by the chemicals that you eat and it is creating decay. *Decay is killing you.* You are decaying from the inside out. You do not see how this is and yet you are told constantly by your doctors how you need more fiber in your diet to sweep the colon because colon cancer is on the rise. Colon cancer is not only on the rise, it is growing so rapidly that you are blocking the entire body and your decay is spreading and cancer is growing in all areas of you. Stop the spread of cancer in your body. Cancer is malignant and spreads when it is fed, and you are decay and cancer is decaying tissue and cells. Get it? You are killing you from the inside out! Stop this nonsense and begin to rinse out your colon. You will not wish to see the results of what you have done to your own bodies and most of you do not wish to be shown or even know that you are decaying. You don't want to stop your fun long enough to "look" at what you have done to your own bodies.

Stop and take a good look. You are decaying so quickly that you are buying more and more medicine and oh how I wish you would stop poisoning your bodies. And each time you snort cocaine or pop a pill or take a drink or smoke a cigarette it offends God. It offends me because you are putting your drugs into a cell in the body of God and I do not wish to see this, and I cannot stop you because so very long ago I decided to allow you free will to return to me on your own. You are like an unruly child who has run away from home and I cannot call the police because free will is in charge, and the police can do nothing in the face of free will. Clean out your colon and save your life... please. Save you to allow others to save themselves. If you concentrate on you and effectively clean you out, you will affect millions by your vibration. One cell vibrates so rapidly once it is clear, that it begins to activate other cells and each new clean cell reacts in the same way. Clear you and you start millions on their way.

So, you do not believe that I am the real God. You see me as part of something spiritual or even supernatural but not as God on high, creator of all and beginner of all. So now I must convince you that I am God on high and not simply someone's subconscious or someone's spirit or someone's own imaginings.

How can I convince you that this *is* me and that you are *in* me and not outside of me? Let's see, maybe we will get together and have a party and I could appear to all my faithful readers. Yes, that would be nice. God could appear, but then if I appear in human form there will be those who don't believe, and those who do believe will shoot those who don't believe and I will start another holy war. Of course, this would be after much shouting at one another to convince each of you who is "right" and who is "wrong." You spend so much time arguing and not convincing, and then killing and still not convincing. This seems to be a pattern with you. Speak your mind and tell your side and if they don't believe you, you must criticize them. And if criticizing them does not convince them (or at least shut them up so you won't have to hear their view) then you shove your ideas down their throat with support from friends who see as you do. And if this fear badgering does not do the job, you convince them how "wrong" they are by showing how many agree with you. And of course, when they come back with supporters of their own we have a real challenge, and now the idea seems to be to make the biggest and loudest noise.

Ah, protest and demonstration, what a joke! God sits here and watches you badger one another with your beliefs and then you get upset when you are not believed and you begin to argue with everyone. All of a sudden everyone is "wrong" but you. You threaten those who do not believe as you do and you push at those who do not wish to make a stand, until they feel guilty about doing nothing - and you are simply *hiding in fear*. You do not wish to be disbelieved because you read this disbelief of you as rejection of you, so you gather support to help calm your own fears that you are not right. And now we have groups of you who travel to shout your rage and anger in areas where you not only do not live, you do not know who does live there, and what their values are, and it is really none of your business.

Stay at home and make love not war. This is what you are doing. You are going into a battlefield each time you pick up a picket sign and begin to march and protest. Write letters if you must but give up this form of doing battle. How can you change the world for better when you don't even know what better is? Stop shouting at one another about *your* rights and allow all to be right. This is nonsense and I wish you to stop. You may change the world by changing *you* - not the guy next door, or down the street, or in the next country. Your life will become better by changing you. No one is infringing on your rights. Allow all to be and you will be allowed to be. You create your own world and you are responsible for what you have drawn into your world. And when you learn to accept this and then change it, you will be happy and you will not "feel" the need to prove anything to anyone.

Did you ever see happy, enlightened people protest? You are destroying one another with your angry words and thoughts and even prayer. Your prayers are very dangerous at this time. Stop praying for the failure of others! There are no others. There is only one God! One body in here... this is it and this body that is God is now speaking to you through this channel and asking you to stop killing! You are killing us. Our body. The body of God. Stop killing one another because you are killing you by doing so. I love you, and I do not wish to add to your fear, but this has gone too far and must stop.

The decay of hate and anger is spreading like cancer and it is very contagious. Please begin to think peaceful, loving, enlightened thoughts and do not shout your beliefs at any. This is not a test tube where the biggest voice wins all. The biggest voice will spread the decay fastest. Slow down and look at who you are and what your motives really are. When you begin to really see you, you will see how fear is motivating each of you - you want to be part of something or just accepted - you want to be heard and respected for your views, or maybe you simply want to help and do what is good so others will not suffer. And I tell you now that *this is your own fear.*

Stop and really see your mirror. What are you afraid of? Are you afraid that you will suffer? Are you afraid that the government is taking over? If you are motivated by fear, you are motivated by Satan. Let go of this hold on fear. When you let go of fear you will be safe. Nothing will occur in your life that is not desirable if you let go of your hold on it. I will not put up with this brutality for long. It is not good for God to experience, and it is killing you. I see only "one."

So, now you are wondering how God will treat you when he learns that you have been killing and fighting and shouting-at and hating others in this body, and I will tell you. God will love you and cherish you and even hold you in place long enough to straighten out this mess you have begun. God will not clean up your mess for you and God will not do your work but God will work with you. God will hold you in place until you are capable of loving you - to the extent that your energy field becomes powerful enough to hold your own position in this universe. God will not punish you because God does not wish to punish nor to judge. So I will simply say, "you are forgiven" as I did with Liane, and that will be that; no big trauma, no big penance and no big sorrow. Let's vote for joy and enlist in happiness and sign peace treaties and sing of love, and forgive-and-forget and live happily ever after - no sorrow, no regret and no disappointment in receiving. We will know that tomorrow will be better and that our future will be bright, and that our future will hold ascension and glory and light.

So, stop fretting over God punishing or judging, because I tell you now that no such thing is possible. God does not judge and God does not punish, so it is time to wake up to the fact that God is good and kind and forgiving and love. You will not find anyone who will love you better than I because I am God and I *am* love. You are loved unconditionally by the king of love, and now you know. I do not care if you are a vagabond in the gutter with no future... you are lovable and loved by God.

Roll up your sleeves and dig in and *accept* me. And clean out you and we will create paradise from this moment on; no big army of angels, just you and I - you and God, God and you - "one," together forever, as one with no separation. Come back home and allow me to help you see the path homeward. Do your enema. It is not the only way back to God, however it is most effective and most efficient and especially speedy. This is the fastest technique yet discovered. Others have used diet and fasting for thousands of years - eat only fruits and vegetables and "clear." This is a good place to begin, however the amount of chemicals in your intestinal tract and colon is so huge that you cannot sweep it out.

When you go to your library, ask to see books on colon care and colon health. Ask for material and information on the amount of destruction going on in the colon. Colon cancer information should give you a good idea of what is going on "in" you. When you receive this information ask for photos on healthy colons and you will find that they do not exist. There is however, information and x-rays on poor, collapsed and mangled colons. Most of you have a mangled colon and if you have your own x-rays taken you will see how badly collapsed you are. So don't take God's word for it. Go read and see for yourself and while you're investigating take a few moments to look up autopsy reports on the amount of debris found in the colon at death. I believe you will find this most shocking and even unbelievable. You will not wish to believe what you read so I suggest you check out several health books to be certain that you convince you.

This is all for now as Liane does not wish to write a biology text and I don't wish to impose this task on her. You may do your own research and then you will wish to thank me for showing you how to save you.

You do not wish to become extinct and you do not wish to save you; so now we are at a standstill. How is it that God almighty can speak to so many at this time in your history and so few will listen? You are so sure that you have all the "right" answers that you do not believe that I am God. You sit and read this and you find it interesting and even informative, and sometimes amusing; but you will not *allow* this information to be the word of God. You are so deep in fear of being fooled that you cannot "see" the light when it shines for you. You are so confused with who you are that you will not allow me to be who I am.

Why would God contact you two thousand years ago and then stop? Okay, this seems to be your belief – "God decided we were running amuck two thousand years ago and he sent us his son to clear a path for him and never again return. He chose to become the kind of ruler who stays away. He doesn't want to mess with the "little people" so he hangs out in heaven with saints and angels and even kings and great leaders. God is too busy to buy a car or spend some time with our problems. God doesn't care how we dress or if we watch violence on television every day. God doesn't get involved in what we do behind closed doors, and he certainly doesn't care that we can't find employment or make ends meet, and he certainly would not get involved in health and politics and our love life." So, what would this God of yours get involved in?

He seems to be very *uninterested* in his children. How can you see me as so unloving and unavailable and uncaring and even unkind? This is God. I am speaking to you now and I am God, and I do not believe it so remarkable that I should have concern for your welfare. Be you green or black or yellow or red or white or short or tall or dumb or not, you are *part* of God and I do not ignore any part that is me. I am God and I am certain that someday you will begin to accept this and soon others will write and converse with God. And one day someone will walk up to you and say, "Hi, I write books for God" and you will say, "So what, big deal, all of us can." So how is it so remarkable now? This is a first. God has not written freely through any of you before, so of course you will not accept. And soon there will be others and you will begin to wonder if maybe... just maybe there may be something to this. And then others will join in and you will follow. There must be a majority who believe before you will follow however.

You see, you're no fool and you won't be made to look the fool by standing up and saying "I believe," because you have no trust and little faith and absolutely no courage. You wish to play it safe and you are living in your fear and mistrust, and when everyone else goes out and proves this to you, then you will listen. You are so afraid to live, that you will not speak your own mind when you do believe. You have lived in a state of denial for so long that denial is at the bottom of your fear. When you begin to admit that you do not have all the answers and that you have not done such a great job living on earth, and you begin to accept that you need help, you will receive help. Ask and you will receive. No special technique. No bending and bowing and scraping. You simply ask God to help and it will be done.

Do not judge God and do not judge you. You are important and I do care and I want only the best for you. You are like the confused alcoholic who will not admit that he has a problem. And if anyone else should imply that you need help you become arrogant and defensive - and heaven help the person who makes these suggestions. You are so afraid to live that you are shutting down your emotions and dying early deaths. You are playing it safe like you have no choice. You *protect* yourself at every turn and you build walls and turn around and build another wall. And soon you will be all walled in, and your fear is *"in"* you and you will sit and decay behind your walls of fear.

And God is here and I am reaching out to show you that I care and tell you how I love you, and you are too afraid to believe that this is me. If God worked with and through his children two thousand years ago, why not today? What was so special about those people? They killed and raped, and incest was common among them. They even carried guilt and fear, and worshiped idols and demons, as you do on earth now. So, what's so special that God would choose to communicate so often in biblical times and not in modern times? I will tell you. They were not so buried in their fear. I could get through to them. Chemicals and other toxins and poisons were not yet discovered, and so when I spoke they had less blocking their source to me or from me. How can they be any more in need of me than you now are?

    I am writing through this girl to tell you who I am and how all works in your own words and with as much simplicity as I can. I wish you to begin to know that *I am God*. Now I very easily could send a savior and you would assuredly lock him up. I could easily speak *through* Liane and she would be carted off to an institution, so I decided to write to you. My words on paper are quite effective and you will read at your own speed, and when frightened you will put this down. When angered, you may also put this down. In the case of a spoken word, you put up your defenses and argue and want someone to prove it to you. With written material, you can argue with yourself and no one is on the other side to try to prove to you or convince you.

    You are so afraid to change that you hold tightly to your belief system and even what hurts you. You are not meant to be in so much pain. You are like the battered wife who will not leave her husband because she has accepted her lot in life and learned how to deal with pain, and if she should leave, she is afraid of what may come her way. You are cowering in fear and you do not wish to be frightened, and so when new ideas are given you turn away and say, "That's crazy, don't tell me that because I won't buy it." Stop being so afraid. You are fear at its most powerful because fear has such a grip on you and you don't even know it.

You will wish to know that Liane and I are not going to give up on you. Liane has not once asked for help in this project and she continues to write for me and I will wish to see each of you have such faith. She is seen as different and not accepted by some, but she knows this is me. She has her days when she wonders if she is okay or sane, but most often she "knows" and she will continue to write books for God until some of you begin to take over for her. She will wish to speak to me now concerning her love life so I will now close.

So, now I have you wondering once again, how can this be? How is it that God almighty, God on high, the universal consciousness, would invest so much time writing to us, the people of planet earth?

This is why. You are me. You are part of me and you are my own energy and thought, and you are in danger of annihilating you, which is me. Stop trying to understand how or why I would contact you and begin to listen and change. You are not the only problem that I have, however you are my weakest link and so I begin where help is most in need. You are the power source of yourselves and yet you are powerless at this time. I will put you back on track and even heal your wounds. You do not wish to be crippled and I do not wish to be hampered and cut off from a part of myself.

You have each had a part in this - and to heal, you will each recover. No one is left out or left behind. No one will 'not' be saved and no one will 'not' be healed. You may take longer than your neighbor, or you may be part of my "A" Team, but you will heal. You will come home to God. You will each ascend and become part of this God force from whence you came. I am the great "I Am." I am God and I started it all by contemplating my own existence, and before I realized the extent of me, I was separating and moving my own self. Now I see how this has created problems for parts of my self and I wish to reverse what has taken place. This is the time of the second coming. God comes to you in written form and shows you how to live and "be."

You will learn to love by simply "being" who you really are. You will learn to care by seeing who you really are and you will learn to trust by letting go of who you now are. You are now Satan. You are fear at his most powerful. You do not trust any and you love even fewer. What you call love is, in most cases, those you call "relative," and in most cases they are not liked or loved. They are accepted because they have association through blood, which is silly because you all come from the same source, and if I were to draw your family tree you would see how you are "all" related and come from them. So, what you do now is to love your relatives and allow a few others to share in your lives, but only if they agree with you and your views. You do not know how to love. You fear so many differences that this fear blocks love. How do you unblock love? You clear fear. How do we clear fear? Right... enema.

Now, when you begin to walk away from fear you will have some confusion. You will walk into the light and you will feel as though you have lost someone dear, and you have. You have let go of fear; fear of rejection, fear of loss, fear of the unknown, fear of lack, fear of surprise and even fear of pain. Now, when you let go of fear, you let go of a big part of you. You have carried this baggage for such a long time and now it is gone, and psychologically you miss this part of you. You miss the old dependable you; and now you are this new person who does not have fear and acts irresponsibly, because this new you does not worry where most people worry. And this new you does not hesitate to pick up and do or go spontaneously. And this new you begins to quit his or her job and starts all over again - and even in some cases carries on like there are no problems in the world. And we all know how silly that is. But this new you simply will not see anything as a problem, and of course this will not sit well with those who believe in big traumas.

So once you begin to leave your fear behind, you begin to miss the part of you that is missing. This is your baggage. The stuff you have carried from lifetime to lifetime and it has been a part of your subconscious for so many lives that you do not wish to part with this old you. And you may come to a point where you are sad and lonely and even a little depressed, and it is just you letting go of fear and mourning your loss. So I wish you to keep going and not let this confusion upset you. You will soon pass into a new area of thinking and you will be most happy that you unloaded your burden of fear.

So, take a long hot soak in a tub and say, "Thank you God, for taking this load from me," and go on about your work of becoming God. You will not wish to be alone and you will only "feel" alone, but I am here, and so are your angels and even those who are part of you living on another plane in a separate but parallel reality. So do not be afraid that you have done something wrong or gone too far or even made a mistake. You will wish to know that you cannot make a mistake. All roads lead to God and all mistakes are simply detours to show you new insight.

Do not be so hard on you for being you. You will each come to a place on your way home to me that is most difficult, and I will not be with you until you make your choice to be with me. This is not to say that I leave you; I do not. I simply wait to see how you will choose and who will win, God or fear.

❧

So, now you believe that this job ahead of you is a big one and you believe that you will never arrive at heavens gate, and I wish to inform you that you have already begun your journey. When you read and think and begin to reprogram your old ways into new more advanced ways, you are moving toward awareness and light, which is heaven. When you first begin to see who you are and how you tick, you will wish to be in the lead, as you will see that not *all* other 'you's' are with you in this project. You may wish to guide the rest of you gently and lovingly.

Whenever there is a part of you who does not wish to comply, you will know that 'that part' carries the greatest pain and confusion. All parts are equal in that *all of you is light*. When you begin to communicate with other parts of you, you will find that some begin to give misinformation and will even go so far as to frighten or threaten you. You will listen to these threats and you will not *fear* what is being said. When you fear these parts of you, you are simply fearing you. Know that *all* parts of you have access to your subconscious and know what frightens you most. *We all have fear on earth.* There is not one among you who does not hold fear. So, when you begin to communicate with other you's and you receive an answer that "no, we are not light, we are Satan," I wish you to love this part of you. You are not evil and there is no such thing as evil possession. Possession takes place only at your invitation. When you invite other parts of you to communicate, they are so anxious to do so that they leave where they are hidden and begin to surface.

Now, the problem that most often occurs is in the energy release. These parts of you are so powerful in some cases that they will literally move your body.

In the case of my pen, she was moved at night when her fear of darkness compounded her fear of being lonely. She was molested in childhood which she interpreted as being used but not loved or wanted. So her subconscious buried these episodes and she grew up normal... she thought. Now that her channeling and professional hypnosis have revealed how she was treated in childhood she can see a destructive pattern in her relationships - subtle but destructive. So now her subconscious is being invited to open up and communicate and she begins to channel Satan... so she believes. He said some pretty bad things and she was sufficiently frightened out of her wits, and she got on her knees and promised God that she would never again channel - and as you can see she did not keep her promise or God would not be working through her now. So, she thought she channeled Satan and of course Satan is simply fear energy, but what she had really done was channel a little five year old girl who was so afraid of being left alone after abuse that she had grown into a monster. And this is what you on earth call evil. Evil is energy that is in its wrong place and will move mountains to be set free. No monsters, no big evil sinister beings, just simple little children who were misunderstood and mistreated.

And who misunderstood and mistreated them? You did. You punished you for your sins and now you have grown into a festering wound. And when someone begins to go into altered states and release this growing pain and pus you yell and scream possession and demons, and yes you see spirits leave at exorcism and yes they do. They are fear at its most powerful. They leave in a group and you see this as a form or shape and you relax because the evil spirit has taken its leave of possessing another body. This possession is not taken on by the spirit or energy; this possession is done by you. You push evil to the bottom of your mind. You create evil by allowing it to be. It is not evil it is simply energy.

When you begin to release your hold on judgment you will no longer have evil in your world. You look at a situation and you judge this situation, and in judging it as bad it reacts as bad. So, do not judge you nor anything that you do. You will wish to know that to love and accept *all* parts of you is best. When you are punished as a child you begin to grow toward punishment. You do wrong - you are punished, so you no longer carry guilt about your wrong doing because you paid. You were put in pain so now you are forgiven. This belief in "pain in exchange for forgiveness" is so strong among you that I cannot convince you that you are God and not meant to be punished - not ever.

So, now you believe that this is law and that all wrong doers must be punished. And I tell you now that this is not so. You do not *know* who is doing wrong so how can you judge? Stop this nonsense and love instead of fearing. You do almost everything in your life out of "fear of." Fear is so strong on planet earth that you need one big giant exorcism, and hopefully you will not go through with it. This is this information you constantly receive concerning earth changes in the years ahead.

Clean out you and you will release your own demons and buried childhood traumas. No big deal - evil has no power. Only when you *fear* something do you give it power. When you communicate with these parts of you and you find them so strong, you may wish to request that they state their grievances and allow you to keep control of your body. Make a deal with them; it's only you... hidden, buried, painful memories who wish to surface in order to make room for the light. They see a way out and they wish only to get out. *You* have made them your prisoner, so of course they will not trust you.

In the case of Liane, she was certain she was dealing with something separate from herself. She slept with her bible on her bed and put salt in the corners of her room; anything to keep the demons away. She was doing battle and it was unnecessary. She could have discussed the entire situation with Satan and discovered that her Satan was simply a very emotionally charged 'fear energy' of about five years old (a child will scream and shout and a frightened child will do whatever is necessary to get "out"). And her little self from childhood was buried so deep that Liane (the adult Liane) would not even admit in her *own* mind that these abuses had taken place. Had Liane been aware of this information, she could have written for this little girl who said so bolding, "I am Satan." And Liane could have helped to release her instead of fighting with her. Love and understanding is always better than a duel. Liane however, was teaching herself to overcome fear of the unknown and she has done well with this lesson.

I wish you to be patient and kind and extremely gentle when dealing with all parts of you. There is no evil spirit and no one is here on earth except *you*. You are all there is, no outsiders, no invading spirits. *It's all you* and you are all God.

Now, when you begin to feel the difference between love and fear, you will begin to know who you are. The biggest difference seems to be that when "in" love, you choose to "fear" that you are not good enough, and this causes you to become fearful that he or she will leave you. You do not wish to remain in fear so I am now teaching you to let go of fear. To fear is to hate your own self. When you hold fear you are rejecting you. You are thinking and believing that you are not good enough, or that you do not deserve this love that is being relished on you. You believe that you are not deserving, and so you create un-lovability, and eventually destroy love for yourself. This of course, is all done without your conscious knowledge because you have no idea (on a conscious level) what makes you, you. You don't know what events from childhood, or even past life, are pushing you forward and driving you to destructive patterns of behavior. You are so uncertain of who you are, that if you were to hear under hypnosis you might not believe.

This was the case with my pen. She was told repeatedly in her channeling and under hypnosis, and with the gradual process of opening her subconscious she was able to recall some memories of child abuse without the aid of hypnosis. This process was very gradual and took several months, and over a period of two years she finally began to "accept" what she was. You do not wish to "be" you because it is too painful, so you bury old pain in your subconscious and you say to yourself "I will not think about this, it is too embarrassing." And so you shut down part of you and this is how you are denying yourself. Denial is at a point in its developmental stages where it is overcoming you. You are more shutdown than you are turned-on. More dark than light. More fear than love.

So, we must make you *all* light once again, and this can be accomplished by you being *all* of you. You do not all hide your own experiences from yourselves as Liane once did. Some of you are very aware and often think about your past pain. You do however; have past life experience that compounds these experiences, as most often you deny part of you in order to handle your own thoughts about your painful experience.

In your search for balance and equal opportunity for all parts of you, you have developed a system where by you "judge" a situation. Then you sentence either one or all participants in this situation. Then you hand out your verdict and live by the rules you have set down to control this relation with these participants. No one will break your rules because each participant knows that you have judged them as wrong for their part in this experience. And of course they feel better knowing that you are somehow restricting your flow of love to them; because they believe in punishment and this is how you have chosen to punish them (unconsciously of course). And of course you feel better because you too are being punished, and it's all because "you" judged this situation and took action to prevent it harming you again. When you give your love in limits and restriction you receive love in limits and restriction. What you are giving is exactly what you are receiving. Give love openly and freely and you will receive love openly and freely.

Now, for those of you who believe it is best to change others so they do not hurt another, I wish you to know that this is none of your concern. You take care of you and I will take care of others. They are all God and I am influencing each part of myself and moving all to the light. You do not understand this nor do you accept this. For now I will give you a very good rule to live by. *Live and let live.* Do not take on the responsibility of other cells within my body. This is not your job. You are not in charge and I do not expect you to teach others when you yourself are blind to what is. This is a case of the blind leading the blind; and instead of one blind cell stumbling and moving, I have two who are falling and crashing into one another and arguing over who is right and who is wrong.

Do not override the will of another. This is important. Do not tell another how to live and do not tell another how to react and do not tell another how to respond. You are acting out "your own" personal pain and hurt. Your opinions are all based on your own hurt and pain and fear, and when you make your rules into a guideline for others, you are giving them your judgments, based on your debris. You do not know who you are or even what you have done in past life. How can you sit in judgment of someone else when you do not *know* who you are? *Do not judge any as wrong.* You are not wrong ever and I wish you to begin to see all through the eyes of compassion. Once you loved without rules as to who was lovable, now you do not know even kindness. Give up this incessant need to be right about everything. This is simply your ego which is controlled by fear. If you do not begin to listen, your ego will take over this planet and earth will be ruled by the anti-Christ.

I do believe this is a good time to suggest you read our first four books before reading this material. I have written four books before this and they contain important information and are necessary in order to comprehend this information. You are not "aware" of what I am saying without first opening your subconscious. You may think you know, however this information has been given in an order that will effectively trigger release within the subconscious, and it is very important that you do not skip books. Begin at the beginning and you will "see" the benefit.

So, for those who are my fifth graders, I welcome you back for more enlightenment. I do hope you are enjoying God's books. It has been a long time since God had the opportunity to speak his mind so freely and I appreciate the use of Liane and her body. She will soon see others begin to do God's writing and this will make her very happy. You will wish to be in class tomorrow as I discuss your love life further. God is now a dating service and God wishes all to love freely and especially openly. Most of you fear being in love, so you do not trust saying "I love you" publicly. You do not wish others to see your pain if you are rejected, so I will now work with you until you learn to love openly and without fear. I do love this part of your schooling. For now I will say adieu and my love to you each.

God

Note: I have a rather large dictionary printed in 1935. This dictionary is over 2,300 pages and shows the definition of adieu as: "a farewell, or commendation to the care of God; as, an everlasting adieu." I just thought that was really nice and wanted to share it with you.

You believe that you do not deserve love for many reasons, one of which is the opportunity to become human. You have chosen to be human and inhabit form, and this form that you inhabit is not to your liking. You find yourself too thin or too fat or just a little short, or maybe, too young or a little over the hill, or maybe you look good but your hair is not right and your teeth are not white and pretty. So, you judge you and criticize yourself and this gradually destroys any belief in beauty and self-love and admiration you may once have had for you.

You are not so unlovable as you believe. What is unlovable is your fear of love. It is impossible for love to find you when you are so busy "fearing" love. Love is not only feared, *you* are feared. When you fear rejection you are telling you how you do not deserve love, and to say that you do not deserve love is to say that you are unworthy. And when you constantly *think* fear and rejection you program you to expect fear and rejection, and what you teach your subconscious is what you will receive back from your subconscious. You are a big computer and what goes in is what comes out. So, how far back does your computer programming go? You bet... all the way back to God force - and God separating by pushing at you until you left out of fear of separation, and now you are leaving one another out of fear of separation.

This separation is based on differences of opinion and religion and life style and even sexes. You find it difficult to spend your life with a man if you are woman, because man is acceptance and denial at its best. Man accepts all into his "mind" then releases his decision based on mental stimulation, while woman is receptive and denial of emotion. She will "know" immediately that she "feels" love, and then will deny it to herself as she fears pain of rejection. He will wait for more data then he too will deny love in favor of fear of rejection.

You are all so hung up in your fear that you are missing the good stuff. When you begin to live and love in the moment, you will see a new you. You will not fear that if you say "I love you" he or she may run. You feel I love you and you express what is felt. This is called spontaneity and is very good. You have forgotten how to just do as you feel. You have lived by rules and regulations for so long that you no longer like surprises and spontaneity for yourselves. You will wish to return to this form of living for your future. You will learn to "go with the flow" without warning or preparation or even a second thought. If it sounds good and feels right... go for it.

So, this is a good time to learn to be spontaneous and to learn to "go with the flow." If you cannot learn to be flexible you will not learn to love freely. Love does not "hold on" and love does not imprison. Love is free and freedom is flowing, and love set free flows to you and through you and back again. Never control love. Never control the ones you love and never let go of you. You will wish to know that when you hold "onto" another for your source of love you are giving your power to them, and rendering yourself a helpless victim who must feed off another's energy. Love them and cherish them and when it is time to move on do so.

Do not believe that all must constantly search for love only to lose love. Love comes to teach you who you are and then love moves to the next partner. And when you truly love you, you will draw your twin soul and you will wish to call all your lovers and say, "I am happy to inform you that I am happily in love and I do not intend to be with any except my twin." And each of your lovers will say how happy he or she is that you have found happiness, as he or she loves you as a friend as well as a lover, and these friendships will last and all will prosper by true love. And this is how it will be - no pain or separation - move on without a fright and when you see your twin soul you will be happy you "let go" of past lovers.

We have a great deal to learn yet in this book. You believe you know best and you believe you are loving and kind, when what you are is confused. You not only do not love, you do not accept love. You begin to see desire and you expect your object of your desire to react in certain ways, and when he or she does not you are quick to accuse and judge he or she. All of a sudden he is not right for you after all or she is not really what you wanted in your life, and you don't wish to waste your time pursuing the wrong mate and so you leave. You stop loving him or her only you never did love him or her in the first place. You had great desire and when he or she did not measure up, you left. You packed your fear of rejection and went on to the next relationship, and if you are lucky you will find a non-threatening partner, one who does not "touch your soul." Those who touch your soul are frightening to you and you run if you can. Some of you are smart enough or have had enough of desire and playing it safe, and you are now ready to risk rejection and more importantly, risk love.

This is where you will each wish to be soon. I wish each of you to do your homework this week. Your homework will be to reach out to someone who is important enough (in your mind) that you fear the threat of pain. I want you to reach out to that special teacher and say, "I love you." This need not be literal. You may give flowers, or send a loving card, or express love in a special "friendly" manner. There are many ways to say, "I think you are very special and you have touched my life." This is your homework and I think you will do well with it.

Let it become fun and games. The more you laugh at your own insecurities, the less they are. Laugh at yourself and you will never feel the pain of rejection. No One can hurt you, only you hurt you.

The Neverending Love of God

First of all I wish you to know that you do not deserve death. You continually punish yourselves with your thoughts until the thoughts you think create sadness then illness, and as a last hope death. Yes, I said hope. You hope for relief from your guilt through punishment. You have been taught to stand up for your rights and be who you are, and when you do, you do not feel good about you because another does not agree with you and so you begin to feel guilty about being you.

You then begin to ease your guilt by punishing you. This may be as simple as berating you or staying away from those you love or simply pushing your energies to their limit. This is a popular form of punishment on earth at this time. We see you judge a situation and move to change this situation to make it "right," and when your plan does not work you begin to wonder if you were "right" in the first place and then guilt overcomes you and you promise yourself to be good or better next time, and of course you have already begun to punish you by putting information into your computer that says you are bad. You are not bad. You are not wrong and you are not right. You simply are existing in a very confusing state.

You don't *know* who you are or how you got here and you are trying to convince yourself to be perfect and there is no perfection only in that all are perfection already. Every experience in your life is perfect. It is exactly what was meant to be or it would not be. You do not do wrong nor are you stupid nor are you in danger. *You simply are.* And when you begin to really see how this is, you will begin to see who you really are. You are not the only one who is in confusion and you are not the only one who wears a mask to hide your confusion and uncertainty. You are each at a costume ball and you each see what the others expect you to see. And once in a while one of you drops his mask for a brief moment and is seen for what he or she really is. And what is he or she... a child, a small, insecure, frightened, little child who wants so desperately to be loved and appreciated, just as he or she is.

To be loved for the self is a blessing and to love another without restriction or limitations is the greatest gift of all. I will not wish to see you all hiding behind your mask any longer. Drop the pretence and begin to show your sweetness and vulnerability once again. All the world loves a small defenseless creature and will rush to protect you from the big bad world. Allow the child in you to be and see how lovable you become. Note that I did not say allow the brat in you to be. No one likes a whining brat who is conniving and demanding. Do not *use* the child in you, but do allow the child to be. Do not fear that you will be hurt without your mask. No one hurts you unless *you* are doing what *you* requested.

You harm you when *you* wish to punish you for what *you* believe to be bad things that you have done. You do not punish you for things that are *considered* right on earth. You do however; punish you for what is *considered* wrong. Remember how some of you once punished yourselves for eating meat on Friday? And some religious groups still punish themselves with guilt and penance for eating certain meats. This is not a good way to live.

All this guilt and punishment is not good for you, and now that you have punished yourself for years you get upset if you see someone else who does not carry guilt. You scream how abortionists are killing babies and how owners of fur coats are slaughtering animals, so they will feel enough guilt to stop and begin to live the way *you* believe is right for them to live. And this of course is *control* and the more control you have over one another the greater your *fear* of losing control, and the only way to end this cycle of fear and control is to end control-through-fear-tactics. These are occurring in your personal lives on a much smaller scale but it is *all* fear, and all control, and all unhealthy. Let the other guy be! Stop trying to control destiny and stop controlling people through fear.

So, how do we get good results and a better world? *Love Love Love.* Stop hating and fearing and begin to love. You hate drugs and hate pollution and hate death and hate taxes. Stop praying to God and asking me to hate. Your thoughts are prayer and I do not wish to have hate mail in heaven. Begin to see only the good and allow God to take care of the rest. God will love you and protect you from harm if you will *allow* him to do so. You are not to be so hard on you or on the rest of you, i.e., the others - the rest of God - the other cells - your neighbors and lovers and family and passengers on this planet. Give up this need to control and all on earth will fall back into alignment. God does not wish to see you in control. He wishes to see you in love. Stop controlling and protecting and begin to love. Stop hating what you see and begin to see beauty. Hate creates hate, love creates love, forgiveness creates forgiveness and abuse creates abuse. Stop abusing you and abuse will end.

You see how it is? It all begins and ends with you. You are the caretakers of this entire universe and when *you* begin to heal and take on light the universe will begin to heal and take on light. No one is here except you. All parts of you are spread out so that you cannot see the whole, however you will heal the whole by beginning with what you see. "The man in the mirror" is beginning to look at himself and say, "Yes, I wish to be healed." And when that takes place the entire universe will "feel" this healing. Know that it takes just one spark to start the fire and one fire can light the world and beyond. Imagine the entire world on fire from the spark *you* will ignite. It is possible and very probable. We have just begun, but it will not be long before we see good results.

You do not wish to change. You are so sure of *your* ways and your answers and your reasons for doing it your way that you will not give love a chance. My way is love, and to love is to let go of you and become love. To let go of you, you must put aside fear, and as you can see by your attitude towards love, fear is so very important in your lives. Mass hysteria is taking place on earth. Large groups of people believing that *protection* is best and that lying to protect yourself from being seen for your true self is acceptable. You are no longer honest when dealing with love of yourself or others. You do not wish to admit to being in love, and when you do, you do not trust that love will last so you begin by discrediting what you have.

Start by seeing only the good. You all appraise your true love before you decide to buy. He or she must "measure up" and be acceptable. Acceptability means fitting in with what all believe to be good and acceptable and being acceptable means fitting in with what is considered "right" on earth. So, if he or she does and says and reacts properly they are accepted and even allowed to receive your love. And the moment they become unacceptable they are out. No more love is given. He or she has disappointed you and must not "receive" from you. Disappointment is in your own mind. You create a picture of how it should be and when it is not you shout how they fooled you and you begin to retrieve your love to use in another time on another subject.

God does not wish to intervene in your ways, however I do believe it is best to let go of what is not working. You have not done such a good job of "acceptance" on earth. "Live and let live" is no longer fashionable. Changing ideas and places and things is the new creative force. "Do not give it a chance to grow" seems to be a motto. Not that you obviously care to change or even think you need change. Change on planet earth is limited to "if I can do it, you can too" or, "if others can so can you." You are not changing for the best. You are limiting and stifling the best. You won't even give the best a chance because you are so busy "fixing" everything that is wrong with everyone and everything.

You do not receive a license to change others simply because you did something for you that made you feel better about you. Stop putting yourself in the position of God. God does not judge and you are taking on this role for yourself. God does not punish yet you punish yourself and you inflict guilt and mental punishment on those who do not see it your way. You do not wish to see the love and goodness in all. You are so full of debris and darkness that you cannot see the light. You are seeing through distorted vision and you are making distorted judgments and you are making mistakes about what is best for you.

So, what does a man do when he no longer has vision? He must trust others to guide him. In this case it is best to trust God and the angels. Go within and ask for guidance. Your neighbor is so busy with his own debris that he cannot help you see any clearer. Your professional and sophisticated leaders are also busy dealing with their own darkness. Trust you from now on. Trust your decisions and your own judgment of what is best for you. You will create greater confusion for yourself by listening to others who are just as distorted as you.

You will begin to "receive" clearer and clearer messages as you become a clear receiver by cleaning out your system and allowing the light in. The light vibrates quite rapidly and will shock you at times. This is to say that when you "receive" great amounts of light you will get shook up; vibrated; become moveable, flexible, and of course confused. You will feel like a snow scene in a glass ball, and when the light comes in, it vibrates and shakes you up, and the snow flies and settles into the eliminatory system of the body and eventually passes through the body and leaves the body.

You will wish to know that a big dose of light can cause disturbances in the body for several months. With the aid of enema you may find that release and relief come quickly, and the waiting time seems to be several weeks and not months. The light is important for you at this time, as you are so attached to fear that you no longer have room for light. You sound off like you are full of bright light and this is simply ego telling you how you are best and you know what is best and you will not be fooled by others.

So, we have what you call a catch twenty-two here. How do we know the true identify of light and how do we know how to be light and how do we know how to and whom to trust? For some this is quite simple. Trust you. Trust that you are God and that you are being led by God and you will do well. You will not find it necessary to lock into a certain belief pattern or even to follow certain rules. There are no rules to becoming God. So, why enema if we can do it another way? The best source of information is received through clean pipes. You cannot channel crystal clear water through a muddy pipe and expect to receive crystal clear water. You receive what you are and you *are* what you eat and what you think.

Since you do not know what you have fed yourself, I suggest you begin a study of food preservatives, chemicals and sugar. Start to look closely at what you eat and what goes into what you eat. You may receive information through your own authorities as to the amount of "safe" chemicals that go into you. There is "no" safe chemical. Chemicals are never safe "in" the body. They have their proper place and it is not in you. You will wish to know how much of what you eat is actually what is on the label. You will find that many products are simply by-products which means that they contain a wide variety of something similar to what you believe you are eating, or in some cases, what you are eating is not at all what its title is. Some cheeses are not cheese and some chicken is not chicken. Poultry is a wide range of birds and poultry by products are often many parts of these various birds. Sometimes you eat feathers and hair and beaks and rodents, and if you request consumer information you will see some of this. Not all is told of course, but you will begin to see how you do not eat what is good for you. You will wish to know that chicken is not meant to be eaten and neither is beef, so you will of course avoid these two animals for now. God does not wish to explain, however I will tell you that these animals have emotions and carry fear and toxins and debris, and you consume them and their fear, and you add to your own darkness.

Do not judge others or try to tell them how or what to eat. You are the only one I am working on - you, not him or her or Suzie or Tommy. You are the student and you are reading this material and you are not to push this information at others just because you have now found your answer. Do not push any to change and do not push you to change. Ask for guidance to change. Ask to be guided to change and it will be done. Nothing is overnight and nothing is healed without first wanting to be healed. He or she will not respond to therapy if the will to heal the self is not there. Go on about your life and allow them to go on about their lives. We do not create a prison where we have rules and a certain standard to live by. We create heaven on earth and this is based on trust and centered in faith.

Faith brought you this series of books. Faith can save you from yourselves. There is no one out there waiting to get you. It's all you waiting to punish you and you don't know why you do this nor what you have done wrong. "Judgment" says you must be punished and judgment is your own belief in right and wrong. Let go of this belief system. Nothing wrong ever occurs. Right does not exist and wrong is nothing but a word that is misused. When you let go of right or wrong you have only "is." What is - not what is right; not what is wrong; simply *what is*. You will not wish this confusion over judgment to continue to rule your world. Let go of the use of these two words and begin to allow "all" to simply be.

※

You do not wish to be so hard on those you love as you have been. You have come to a place that is very confusing for you in that you "know" who you love, only you do not realize who you love. This is confusing for you and I will wish to clear your confusion. You love the one you most enjoy and you love the one you most do not enjoy. These are those who are very important to you. You do not find much interest in someone you do not enjoy and you find great interest in someone who is enjoyable or even a nuisance to you. So, you can be certain that the ones you love are those who bring you the most sorrow or the most joy. How can this be? I will try to show you how this is.

First of all, you are energy and spirit, and you mix energy with spirit and you have essence. When essence meets like essence you have a compound that we will call "all you." You become drawn to this other person who is your same essence. You will find that those in your life who do not wish to be with you out of lack of interest are simply not operating at the essence level that you are projecting at. If he or she is interested but not drawn, then he or she is operating at your level but not yet attracted to your force field or your aura. So, if I am God and you are God, how is it that you operate at a separate level than others who are God?

You will wish to know that you are actually different layers of God. God is an onion and has layers. This is not literal of course, so please do not rush out to teach the world that God is a giant onion. Parables have confused you in the past so I wish to clarify whenever I teach in this manner. Now, back to God the onion. God has layers or skins and they resemble an onion and when you have peeled away all the layers what do you have left…? Right… nothing. Oh, but in this case, to have nothing is what we are after.

Confusion and debris have brought about matter which is dense. Density creates thickness or confusion, and thickness is difficult to see through. You must become undense, or transparent, or nothingness to return to God. You must bring down your walls and bare your soul so that soul may "be." Soul is imprisoned behind walls, or debris, or past pain and confusion. Soul wants out and soul will soon request that you begin to "peel" away your debris. Peel your onion and allow soul out. Get back to what you really are which is essence of God, not matter. You are not matter and you do not belong behind or within matter. You are God and you belong in God force and not separated by God or even by walls.

Now, in the beginning I did not know how I separated myself and how I pushed until part of me left. Now that I am "aware" how this has occurred I am ready to clean up my own mess and put God back together again. So, to put God back together again I must first put my cells in order, and of course you are God's cells and you must make this choice to heal, as I do not override your will. So, how is it that God will talk you into healing and clearing and peeling you, the onion. I will do my best to entertain you and intrigue you and love you until you learn to trust that this is indeed me. Then we will have a good time together and we will each know that God communicates with his children and even that God *is* his children.

Now, back to those you love and how you "know" whom you love. You will draw those who are "peeled" to the level that you are peeled. You will each be uncovering lessons to guide you to peel further. You will know you in each of these people if you simply look for your reflection. If you are annoyed by their presence it is your reflection of how you annoy you, and if you are elated by their presence it is your reflection of how you elate you. It is this simple. You *are* who you are looking at. You draw to you what you are and you do not wish to "see" what you have drawn.

You will each find that to look for you in your friends and lovers will show you your way out and back to God. The closer you look for you, the clearer you see. Do not look "at" and judge your friends and loved ones. You are judging you by doing so. You will wish to know that you do not "receive" you well and to look at your mirror is going to allow you to receive you. You are not so confused as you were when you first read God's first book and now that you are reading this, God's fifth book, you feel that you have your answers.

You have come to a place in your education where you believe that you are "aware" because you have begun to see more clearly how *all* actually is. When you learn that your answers are only for *now*, you will see differently. "All" is only now. "All" changes with time and layering. When you un-layer or peel, you become a new you. And each new 'you' has new things to learn to allow you to get to the next layer. So you will not wish to "hold" onto the answers that allowed you to remove the last layer. We start with a new you and I give new information. When you begin to see this, you will understand how constant change *is*. *Is*, is now and now is "being." So, continue to "be" by constant change and you will *be*. This may sound confusing but it is quite clear to me. So, you must clear enough to make this clear to you and you will become me... Get it?

When you are finished peeling you, you will become nothing once again. And nothing is everything, and God is nothing more than everything that is nothing. Now that I have you using your mind I will allow you to use this time to reflect on the lesson I gave you yesterday in class. Did you do your homework and reach out and say, "I love you and you have touched my life" to someone you love? Preferably this was done with one you feel is dangerous to you in some way. You may learn to love *all* parts of you by giving to all parts of you. You *are* all - them too. You will one day know how you fit in and even how I fit in. For now I will leave you with this thought; you are not only God, you are you.

You of planet earth are now in a position to become the son of God and ascend. You have been pretending to be man for such a long time that you do not realize how you are still God.

When I first began to concentrate and expand and move within myself I had no premonition that anything unloving was about to occur. In "being," I *am*. And in being I am now, and in being now, I am not in future probabilities. So for now I will try to explain how this belief in an all-knowing God has come to be. *We are all God.* In being God we are everlasting light, and light is awareness and intuitive knowledge. In "being" first or one and only, it is not possible to have intuitive knowledge which is based on past experience or instinct. You sense, you know, you react. Well, when you are the first or the one and only, you have not before experienced and you are experiencing and expanding in awareness as you go.

So far most of you have good intuitive skills based on instinct which is based on survival skills or past programming. Before you were programmed you were blank, or clear, or a clean slate. Programming teaches us what is good for us or painful for us. We touch a flame and it burns. This information is processed as painful and goes into your computer. God pushed at himself to "see" if it were "all" him or someone else with him and this created many varied responses which became part of Gods unlimited awareness. God did not punish God for pushing at himself as he did not judge this as anything harmful or even dangerous. So God does this investigation of himself and he becomes *more* of himself as he *is* thought, and thought through experience creates more thought energy. Now we have God growing in awareness of himself and gradually he begins to expand and move and separate. Sort of like a giant white cloud that gradually drifts to become part of other clouds and leave parts of himself as he goes.

Now we begin to grow and gather in information about the self. And as I grow I expand and now I have more movement in more of me. So this movement begins to draw my attention and I begin to "see" how big I actually am. And as I move I continually grow, so I am constantly *becoming* God. I am not whole and will never be complete. I am constant and on-going and everlasting and even eternal. However, I do not know "all" of me as all of me is continuously new and arriving and departing. How would you like to be new but old, and on-going but ending? Well, you are. You are me and you do not respond to who you are as you do not know or acknowledge many parts of you. So, what began it all? How did God start and when will God end?

God started with a molecular structure called cell thought. This cell thought has no beginning and will not end. It all started when molecules began to form, and molecules began to form before thought cells were. So, thought cells are actually molecular structures that combine to create action and reaction. Action is the part of God that is known as ether, and ether is "all," in that it is the *"is."* "Is," as I told you yesterday, is a state of being, and being is constant and now, and I *am* now. So, when you think of God you must know that God is the beginning and the end, only we have no beginning and no end. God is now. Now is forever. You will learn how to be happy by living *now*. Now is the beginning and now is the end. Do not love for tomorrow. Do not hate for today and do not wait to "be" until some future, because you are only now.

When I began to see how I was only me and not more, or separate, I began to allow all of myself to be. I will wish to see you recognize that you are all of me and it is best to allow "all" of you to be. For now I wish to thank Liane as she has been uncomfortable during this writing. I will discuss the art of being and isness further tomorrow. Go in peace and God bless you.

Once you began to see how you did not love one another, you began to judge yourselves as not good enough. The only one who did not judge in this situation is God. I did not judge as I did not wish you to be so frightened of yourself, who is me. So, if I did not, and do not judge you for being unkind and unloving, how can you judge you as being unkind and unloving?

You do not know how to accept. Now, acceptance as you see it, is learning to live with or tolerating, or maybe even self-punishment. These are not acceptance. These *are* judgments. When you "decide" to stick it out in a relationship because he or she has been good to you, you are basically judging this situation. You feel that you owe he or she, which is to say that they deserve you or what they want, but you do not deserve whatever it is that you want. Most of you compromise yourselves and this is due to a lack of self-love. Once in awhile you get up on your high horse, or ego and you shout how you deserve better, and actually this has nothing to do with your partner. This has to do with you and how you judge you and your life.

So now ego is screaming for better treatment, and so your partner may consider this a warning that if he or she does not shape up, you will ship out. And so he or she tries to do better, and this is blackmail and even fraud, because the one trying to do better is not being who they really are. And now you have someone pretending to be what you want them to be and no one is going to grow in this situation. So, if you have been telling a certain someone to shape up or they're out, I suggest you change this to "I will shape up so you will love me," and see how quickly they begin to respond to this type of "love" treatment.

You are not to live the life of another nor are you to tell another how to live. You simply let them be who they are, and if this is not possible for you to do I suggest you leave them and explain clearly that it is you and your own insecurities, and not them. This is taking responsibility for self. Do not take responsibility for a body or human that is not inhabited by you directly. Let go of this need to blame everyone else for what occurs "in" your life. You are "in" your life, not he or she and certainly not me. I am not allowed "in" anyone's life these days. How in the world am I going to guide and direct your play for you if you do not allow me on your set? Life is a giant play with all the characters in place as you have asked. You wrote and even created this play for you. You asked each character to be who they are and now you ask why they act a certain way, and this is so ridiculous because you wrote their part for them.

Those of you who have read Miss MacLaine's, *It's All in the Playing*, which was required reading for my students in grade two, will be well aware of how you produce your own life like it's a giant play. Now, for those who do not allow me on the set, you are on your own and will bump into obstacles, and of course eventually everything will be worked out. But, those who allow God on their set will know how to move to avoid certain big problems simply by "seeing" ahead of time what may have been created by taking a certain turn, or moving a certain character. God does enjoy guiding you each and the faster I am "accepted" and allowed to "be" exactly who I am, the faster we get to total peace and harmony. So, to be God is not the greatest but to be God is best. God is all-knowing and all-seeing and all-awakening and even all-loving. Once you learn to accept all parts of God as God, you are accepting God. God does not wish to be a problem for you to solve. God does wish to be loved and accepted.

Now; back to those who are asking their partners to shape up. I will allow you to gently and lovingly ask for help in accepting them as they are. You may not ask them to change in any way; however you may ask them to assist you in learning acceptance of you, which is what we are really learning here. You may explain to your mate or friend how you have insecurities within you that cause *you* to not accept certain traits in another. And these certain traits will no longer be offensive to you once you have learned to accept all of you with love. Your mate will be happy to see that you are finally seeing some of your own problem areas, and will be most loving in this lesson for your own acceptance of you.

So, this is your lesson for today and I wish you each to look to someone you have tried to change, whether it is as small as a phrase you did not care for that they may frequently use, or a big mistake "you" believe they are making in their life. Now, I do expect you to be honest in asking for help and not insinuate in any way that they are actually the one who must or should change. This lesson is for you, not them. You are climbing this ladder, not them. You are the man in your mirror, not them. Now I wish you a good day and happy acceptance of you!

The Neverending Love of God

※

*O*nce you begin to see how simply I have taught, you will begin to see how easily you may learn. You do not wish to be unkind or unloving, and yet it seems to be your nature to get upset with those you are in relationships with. Most of you do not wish to be so unkind and often do not *realize* that this is anger and not simply the other person being impossible. When you become frustrated by someone else, it is to show you how you have anger at yourself, and in using this as a testing ground you may begin to look into your anger and ask yourself why you are indeed angry.

We are never upset for the reasons we believe. It is usually much deeper and much simpler, but because you do not use your powers properly you develop other reasons or answers for your performance, and then you begin to feel better because you have now justified and made your way right. Most often you do not wish to be discomfort-able or uncomfortable with your friends and lovers. Often you wish to be the one who is admired and looked up to and even loved. This is the bottom line. When you blow your cool and get upset, or misjudge a situation and loose control, I wish you to remember that this is simply you screaming for love in the same way that your neighbors and friends and associates scream for love.

When you see giant eruptions of pain and confusion and frustration in your daily lives, reach out and hug that person, or verbally hug that person for God. If you cannot overcome your fears enough to love them for yourselves, then please love them for me. I wish to give comfort to many at this time and I do not have the opportunity to hug unless you allow me the use of your bodies. I will not take advantage of this privilege and I will not return your favor unrewarded.

When you work for God you begin to receive God. God does not wish to go into detail here; however I do wish you to know that I am the "I Am." And when you receive "I Am," you receive the connection that is necessary to start you *back* to your beginning, and your beginning is actually the end. The end is 'always' and the beginning is 'now.' When you begin, you begin the end. When you begin to sing a song, you begin to end that song. When you are born, you begin to die and when you are born again "in" God, you begin to end you and begin a "new" you.

So rejoice at the end because your end is simply my beginning. When I am born again we will have our second coming. No big march across this planet. Just a simple little end with a new beginning.

Now I will begin to explain about love of self. You do not know how to love you. You have spent so many lifetimes loving fear and holding to judgment that you do not know love of self. First off, to love the self first is not selfish, it is selfless. To love you, you must accept you, and to accept, you must remain "in" love, and to remain "in" love is to be light and God.

Now; in the beginning I did not wish to intervene as I did not wish to confuse you further. Now you are at a point in your evolution that is critical and I wish to *guide* you back to God and I wish to share my knowledge and information with you. You see, I have been here waiting for an opening in creation so that I might freely enter. I have not waited for long as I do not experience time as you do. *I am all that is. I am* the beginning and the end and *I am* eternal and *I am* "One" and *I am all that is.*

If you will study child psychology you will see that children form opinions based on judgments concerning love and hate. And any psychologist could sit down with you and show you how your childhood judgments are affecting you now and you would not find this so unusual. Take this one step further and you will see how past life judgments affect this you. You are the sum total of what you believe, and believe me when I tell you how you have no idea what makes you up. You are so packed with judgment that you no longer operate from your true source. You are running off debris and negative judgments and nothing is *"clear"* to you. Become clear and learn to see who you are.

How can I teach you to love you if you do not look at you and see what makes you up? I will teach you to love you by teaching you to accept you, and so far you refuse to accept without proof. You want proof of everything because you have no trust and no faith. Trust and faith come only with love. *If you do not trust, you do not love.* It's this simple. Do not look to God for love of you and do not look to your mate for love of you. Learn to accept you by trusting you and learn to trust you by loving all, and learn to love all by letting go of fear and mistrust. This is your ticket out of fear. Trust God, trust love, trust all.

I know this is a big no-no on earth at this time. Trust was once a positive light. It is now a negative word that is shunned. You are taught from childhood to mistrust. Don't trust strangers, don't trust liars; don't trust people who are important politically and so on. *Do trust.* I am asking you to please trust again. Trust will save you from your fear. Trust God and trust angels and trust you. Don't be so afraid of trust. What you fear most is what you will see. Be kind to you by not allowing your fears to run your life. The bigger your fear, the faster it creates and materializes. Do not give fear power in your life. Cheat fear by trusting others and yourself.

I know it's not easy for you here on earth but maybe it will help you to know that I trust you.

So now I have you wondering how to trust and who to trust and how to overcome your *fear* of trust. Yes, you fear trust. Look around you and you will see how you safeguard against trust. You lock your doors because you don't *trust* that you are safe. You hide your valuables because you don't *trust* that you will not be harmed, and you protect yourselves with fear tactics because you do not *trust* love. You build walls around your heart to protect you. You build gates and walls around your belongings to protect *your* possessions, and you build big walls around your mind to block what you believe to be untruth or trickery.

You are all walled in and walled out. In building your walls of protection you forgot to let the fear out. You are sitting in your home with your gun loaded, and the windows barred, and your doors bolted, and your alarm system turned on to warn you of any intruder, and you are "locked in" with *fear*. He sits with you and he sleeps with you, and he is the Devil. Satan is fear, and fear energy is taking over this planet. When you begin to *realize* who he is and how he works, you will no longer fear him. You will simply let him be, to go his own way. He is trapped and *you* will not allow him to return to become God force once again. *Your* hold on fear is very tight. He does not have a grip on you. You are holding so tightly to fear that you are afraid to release what you have come to know and love. Yes, you love Satan.

You love fear because it is comforting to you, and to comfort you is simply to make you feel at ease, and *all* of you are very at ease about locking and bolting *for* fear's sake. Whatever makes fear happy is what you will do. You have been told often how Christ taught trust and faith. Will you unlock your doors for trust and faith or will you continue to work for fear (Satan)? The choice has always been yours and you have chosen fear. I am asking you to stop worshiping fear. Begin to worship God by moving "into" the light of love. God is love and love does not mistrust, and love does not judge you as too bad, or too almighty, or even too fearful. *Love simply is.* And love waits to enter you and become more of you.

You wish to become God and return to the light. You must begin to trust and to love. Love does not exist in a body that is filled with fear. Fear or love - you cannot have them both. You must choose before you can become light. It is not possible to ascend, nor is it possible to be darkness and vibrate at a speed necessary for survival. All will clear and all will walk with God in heaven and all must choose wisely. You do not threaten your neighbor or tell him he must not lock his door. I am speaking directly to you and not to him. Unlock *your* door.

※

You begin to see how all is not as you believed. Your sense of right and wrong is actually "protection" against others and a way to control others so *you* do not feel threatened. When you begin to release your grip on fear, you will allow others to live their own lives and you will be concerned only with controlling yourself and not others. You have come to a place that is dangerous for you. You do not wish others to kill and yet you kill. You do not wish others to be violent and yet *your* thoughts are violent. You think bad thoughts and believe if you continue to suppress your negative emotions you will be kind and loving. Negative *thought* creates. And negative thought expressed verbally leaves, and negative thought acted upon begins to show you who you are.

So, all thought that is not light or love is dangerous. Negative thought that is suppressed and turned inward will destroy you, and negative emotion will grow from this buried thought. And this emotion will begin to take over your life, and you will wonder what happened when all of a sudden you snap and begin to yell at a loved one. No one enjoys yelling and screaming at others. If you enjoy such scenes you are playing with your own emotions. Screaming is not your natural state, and to convince yourself that it is good for you is not so. You will feel better after screaming because you will have released old trapped emotion.

Do not scream at someone, scream with someone. Go to Disneyland or any "funland" where they give you rides that frighten the screams from you. Scream *with* others and enjoy getting these emotions out. Do not scream *at* others. You only create more negative thought. Do not judge those who scream at you as wrong. Those who scream and yell at others to be heard, are far deeper in their fear and need love, not judgment. So, continue to release and continue to love while releasing. It is not necessary to damage yourself just to get to know who you are and what is in there (in you).

You will wish to know that to love you - you must first accept you, and to accept you - you must first accept others. Let them be and you are letting you be.

Now I wish to tell you a story. This story began two thousand years ago in a very small town called Bethlehem. In this small town I began to do my work. A small child was born and I began to speak *to* him and I began to ask him to learn for God. He did not question this phenomenon, nor did he ask me to prove that *I am all that I say I am.*

So now I am communicating with this child and I find it necessary at times to teach him in very simple stories. A child's mind is very small and does not require complexity. So, now I have my student and he turns into a teenager and he begins to learn the ways of the world, and of course he begins to question what I have taught in his adolescence. All of a sudden he begins to know better than God, and of course this is in part due to his age and what you call puberty.

Now I have a more difficult time teaching him, as he begins to question and no longer simply accepts. His peers are smart and he believes them when they give their ideas of this world, and of course he has answers that were given to him by a voice. How do you know who to trust? This strange voice that has always insisted he is God or others who live on planet earth. You see how this could be quite confusing for any young man. So now I must prove myself often to this young man, and his psyche begins to develop with his growth and he is quite without fear of the unknown. He has lived several past lives and these lives are made available to him in the sense that he might wish to view a scene from one or two past life experiences, especially where God is included or concerned.

So now I have his attention but not his trust and faith. He began to walk his own path, and this is to say that he did not wish to teach what he was unsure he believed. He spoke with Temple leaders and expressed his views strongly at times, and at other times he listened. He listened to hear what others were teaching because he knew he was unsure. He even went so far as to question others who claimed to have communication with God. You see, back then it was not such a big scene if God chose to speak to one, or several of his children. Now he is beginning to "see" how he may just be teaching for God and it begins to dawn on him what a big responsibility this is.

He begins to prepare himself to teach for God and this of course will take some time. He went through a period of cleansing his soul and fighting his own demons and even fasting to clear the body of debris. You see, if you go without eating for long periods of time the body devours everything in it, even its own intestines. You will see that this is not such a good way to prepare to receive God, as it weakens the body to the point of exhaustion and the cells begin to die. And of course God is *in* each cell, and when the cell goes God goes - one cell at a time.

Now back to this boy who is teaching for God. He does not wish to take on the responsibility of speaking for God and so he begins to adjust his mind to be perfect. He believes that to speak for God he must first be perfect and *know* who he is, and so he begins his path to knowledge - knowledge to perfection of his own state of being. He is spending his years growing in awareness and enlightenment, and now he believes he is ready to teach for God. This took a short time in God's eyes and he is now a young man and is willing to *accept* that I am God. He gained insight and wisdom to learn to *accept* God. And now he is teaching for God and of course many call him liar and others walk away from him and still others are upset that he should claim to speak for God. He is accused of treason and he is threatened and he is even called crazy; *all because God wished to communicate with his children.* Not much has changed in the last two thousand years has it?

※

You do not believe that I am God and you do not believe that I would come to you in this fashion. Most of you believe that I am some "part" of Liane's subconscious, or maybe even a future self, or an Angel who is somehow connected to Liane. I tell you repeatedly who I am and you will not believe. You are so afraid to be different and "believe" that you go along with society and disbelieve. You are so certain that to believe that Liane channels God will be a mistake, that you refuse to trust "in" me. You are allowing this information "in" only if it suits you. You are so afraid to trust that you would rather be safe than saved. You would rather wait for proof than begin to clear you now. You would rather die of toxic debris than be made a fool of.

So now we have you wishing to be free and clear and it is not instantaneous. All comes to those who ask. And all comes to those who seek. Seek and you shall find. If you are "looking" for something you will eventually find it. If you search for good health, it is yours. If you search for love, you will receive love and if you ask for faith, you will *receive* what you do not know. You do not know trust and you fear trust will bring you harm. Stop allowing fear to run your life. Allow faith to lead you to trust. Trust is not exactly what you would call a gift if you do not "receive" it.

If I shove trust down your throat, you will be doing out of fear and not out of trust. Trust will come by allowing yourself to change. Change your programming and allow a new you to *be*-come. You do not trust that you have guidance that will help you make "good" choices, and you do not *trust* that love is all that is necessary to survive. If you were to allow yourself to float free of your inhibitions and turmoil, you will see how you are not only happy, you are safe. You believe only in proof, and this time *you* are requested to prove to yourself how all really is possible.

You will not find safety in numbers. You will not find safety by hiding, and you will not find safety in your homes. You will find safety in trusting that you are safe. Safety creates safety, just as love creates love and hate creates more hate. Create safety by believing in safety. You have created danger by believing "in" danger, and look what it has brought you. Look around and see what *you* have created. One single thought has the power to kill. Do not *think* bad thoughts about your life in any way, shape or form. You are killing one another with thought, and then you scream murder at the actor who played the part in your play for you by pulling the trigger, or driving the deadly car *you* are creating with your fear. Stop *using* fear to create and begin to *use* love. Love will allow you to be who you are, and love will allow you peace, and love will allow you more of the same.

You need not question your own thoughts. Simply look at who you are, and if you *see* violence, it is your own violence, and if you *see* hatred it is your own hatred being projected out and reflected back. When you begin to *see* all situations with love in place of judgment, you will be seeing your love projected out and reflecting back. If you are confused, I suggest you return to Book Two and see how your thought creates *your* world for you. You will also find *It's All in the Playing* by Shirley MacLaine to be of great help.

You will see a big change in your attitude and how you view life when you see peace where you once saw conflict, and you see a cry for help where you once saw anger, and you will see the ponies whenever you look for them. Look for the pony my children. You will find what you are searching for. If you prepare for the worst you are creating the worst. If you get a second job just in case, you are telling your computer that you are preparing for failure. If you search for disease you will create disease, and if you lie and tell others you are ill you are telling yourself to become ill. Watch how you create and what you create. Know who you are and don't act as though you are someone else unless you plan on becoming that someone. When you create an invalid or handicap to receive attention, you are literally performing and shaping what you will be. When you begin to scream abuse you are creating more of what you are projecting. If you don't want it in your life don't project it out to reflect back.

Thought is like a prayer - a request to the universe saying "do this" or *"I am* this." Stop programming illness and death. What you ask for is what you get. If you ask for youth you are saying "I am old and I don't want to be." Ask for good health to continue forever. Ask for youth to never end. Always speak as though you are, right now, what you wish for. If you wish for prosperity do not begin to say, "I want to be rich." Begin with, "I am so rich, thank you God." What you believe is what you receive, and God has a real problem getting your gifts to you when you are all so busy screaming for and creating what is not good for you. So, I wish you to do this lesson tonight before sleep. Do not get down on your knees as it is not necessary to humble yourself before God, when you are "part" of God. To bow to God is to receive and create information that says, "I do not deserve God," or "I am not as good as God." So, up off your knees please. Say to yourself repeatedly "I am happy and prosperous and healthy and I wish to continue with this good fortune." Write it, memorize it, and do not forget to *think* it.

This is good for now. You will wish to know that you are not the only one who is requesting peace, and I will be most happy when your requests begin to roll in. Thank you for trusting me enough to share your lives with me, and I wish to continue this correspondence with my children. There, God has just requested his part in this to 'be.'

Loving Light

Once upon a time I did not wish to frighten those who live on earth by my presence and so I kept a silent vigil instead. Now I have no way of keeping silent as my presence has been requested again and again. I do however; hope you will not be upset with me for appearing in written form and asking you to help. You have each been left outside of God for such a long period that you no longer wish to return. I have not judged you nor have I asked you to return until now. Now I am asking and you are saying "No, I don't trust you and I don't believe that you *are* God. God is more powerful and God is more forceful and God would not write books and certainly not books that ask us to enema."

So, how can I convince you that *I am* God without loss of trust and faith? I could appear out of the heavens in a chariot of fire and the government could haul me off as they have with various others who have visited earth. Or I could simply appear to *you*, no one else - just you - and let *you* convince the rest of the world. Do you think you could do that? No, I don't think so either. So, if I were to appear I would do one giant command performance, maybe in the South of France, it's nice there. No, that wouldn't do, because the folks in England wouldn't believe and may start a holy war over the audacity of one country to think that they are so special as to host God's appearance. So, if I appear to one I must appear to all. And once I make this appearance there will be those who *deny* and shout trickery, and of course those who believe will show them how wrong they are to not believe and they will raise their voices and shout who's right and who's wrong. And then anger will take over and God will watch in horror as his own body cells begin yet another war. So, I think I'll just sit here with Liane and write to those who are ready to read about life, and God, and the power of love.

Love is not so much a danger as you believe. Love is a power and at this moment in time love has become a most undesirable power. No one wants to be "in" love, as to be "in" love is considered painful. Here we have a big misconception. Power is good not evil. To *have* power is what you are. You are power, and this power that you hold is energy and this energy is God or love. Do not fear love for you are fearing you... you are God and God does not wish to become fear. Stop becoming fear by letting go of your fear of love. You will not suffer from "real" love. You will suffer only from your fears: "I fear he will not be the kind of mate that I deserve, so I will convince him to change and to see how wrong and afraid he is;" "I do not wish to love her because she wants to change me, and to change me is to control me and who I am. I will not be controlled or I will lose part of me." These are your own fears and you see your mate and his "problems" clearly and so you tell him how he is being guided and affected by his fears and I wish you to look at who you are.

Look at this reflection of you. You are telling him or her how to act and react in a relationship because *you* are so afraid of losing. You have so much fear of loss that you will control and train so that you may "keep" yourself intact. You are afraid of losing part of you to love. You will not settle for a lover who is not up to your expectations, because in your mind this is to settle for less, and of course you know that you deserve the best. I will tell you now that when you learn to love out of love and not fear, you *will* have the best. You will not "see" the good by asking to be shown by another. You will see the good by believing it is. This is good for you to practice. You are not simply in the middle of a big lesson in your relationships. You are in the middle of a big gift. If you do not "see" the gift it is because *you* are standing in mud or debris. Don't scream and shout about your mates muddy feet when it is all your own debris that is blocking and distorting your own vision.

    You will wish to know that you do not know what makes you tick or even why you find certain situations to be undesirable to you, and I will tell you once again that it is because *you* are the one who is trying to control out of your own personal fears. And you are the one who is seeing this situation as undesirable and *judging* it as wrong for you. It is not wrong so stop pretending it is. It is not wrong to become dependent on another. It is not wrong to want another to help you in your life and it is not wrong to be exactly who you are, which is very difficult since none of you seem to realize that *you are love.*

    At times you do not show, or look like love. Love does not say, "I will be happy today because he is good to me and sends me flowers." And love does not say, "I will be sad today because he was distant and unloving and he doesn't want a relationship with me." Love simply says, "I love you, what hurts?" Or, "I love you - how can I help," or "I love you and if you want someone else then that is what I want for you also." Love will say, "I do not wish to take from you or change you. I only wish to give to you. You may do whatever you like and I will not change my love for you. Be you and be happy." That is what love wants for others, not "Be mine and make me happy."

So, you can see how we still have a great deal to learn about love which of course is us, our-own-selves. We are love and love is God and soon we will love unconditionally and we will have our own happiness, even though we believe our happiness only comes from others and their acceptance of us. Love is letting go of fear, and fear is controlling, and controlling is not good for love. "Let go and let God" is a very good saying and will help you if you do believe that God loves you.

---

*O*nce upon a time, I began to assess all that has gone on within me for the last few millennia. Now that I see clearly how *all* have become fear, I wish to change what is. I no longer wish you to live within the power of Satan. When I (God) am with you, you are strong and free from all pain. When I am not with you, you are weak and create chaos for yourselves. *I do not leave you.* You leave me. Fear enters you and I am not "felt" or seen. I am still you as you came from me and you *are* me, only now you are not *expressing* as me. Now you are expressing as pain, or anger, or fear of, or hurt, or struggle, or just nervousness. These are not God. God *is* love and light and awareness and inspiration and knowing how beautiful and talented you are. Love is, simply put, you at your most Godly. Love does not require you to be left outside of yourself nor to put restrictions on yourself. Love does not require you to be more nor less than God. You are God simply by being in your natural state.

Never allow God to leave you or never switch to fear, and you will never see pain or confusion. Know you and you know God. Love you and you love God. When you allow someone else to influence your choices because you feel guilty about how they will see you or accept you or not accept you, you are being "fear of," not love. Be love and allow all to occur or not to occur in your life. You do not come back to God by accepting only what others say is acceptable. You return to God by not being "fear of" at any time. So, when you begin to live *for* you and do for you, you will grow in God's light and love. You are not here on earth to live your life for others and you are not here on earth to please others. You are God and you are here to learn to return to God.

You learn to return by loving the self. The self must come first as the self *is* God and God must come first. When you learn to love your own self unconditionally, you will draw unconditional love of all to you, meaning you will no longer feel the need to live your life to please others or out of guilt of what others might think or even out of guilt of hurting another. You do not hurt someone else's feelings by being you and "going for it" *for* you. You hurt no one by *accepting* the gifts that may enter your life. So often I see you turn your back on what I send out of a need to be accepted by your loved ones or out of guilt that your loved ones will take this situation that you are inviting the wrong way and "feel" hurt. You *never* hurt another.

Each of you create and learn from each experience that you *receive*. And when you begin to carry the worry or concern for others, you are simply taking their lesson for your own. When you do not take or receive a new experience in your life, out of fear of someone you care for misunderstanding you and "feeling" pain because of this, you are stifling your own positive growth and you are stifling their lesson as well. Now, I do not say that to do *for* this loved one is wrong, nor is it right. It simply is.

Do not exist out of shame or resentment or fear of. Exist out of love. Be who you are and allow others to be who they are. You are not here for your own gratification; however you are here for your own love. Create love wherever you go and go wherever and whenever you wish. Do not learn to control you through guilt. Do learn to allow you to move freely and of your own personal choice toward the gifts. You are not meant to be denied and you *are* meant to receive. You receive by giving to the self first. Give until you no longer feel that you are undeserving or undesirable.

You will wish to know that you may receive more than one gift in each lesson and you may lose these gifts, however, you *will* draw another gift (or lesson) to you. You cannot lose as you are now on your path to God. There is no turning back once you begin to *receive* me. I am working with your soul at *your* request and I am receiving you as myself. I will not turn away out of fear of neglect. You may not be aware that I am with you; however I am quite aware that you are struggling to be with me. Don't struggle my children. Be and let be and do not judge your motives nor your actions and you will become love and light once again. Do not be so hard on you for not being perfect. Perfection is a state of becoming and you *are* becoming and are therefore perfection.

༄

You do not wish to be so concerned with how you look that you do not shine. Most of you are so afraid of looking ridiculous, or silly, or just too old, or too young, that you no longer enjoy life. You do not become "involved" as you once did. When young, you danced and sang and ran and jumped and played. Now that you are maturing you believe it to be not such a good idea to sing or dance unless you "feel" that you have a talent for these gifts. Most of you believe that once you mature it is not correct for you to wear certain clothes or act in a "young" fashion. You are permitted to be mature but not old. Isn't it silly how you react to age? You all wish to be young and yet you ridicule those who you believe to be too mature to wear certain styles. And you even criticize those of a certain age who date someone who is much younger or much older. You are so set in your rules that you leave no room for flexibility or free speech.

You accuse one another of speaking kindly of another and then you think unkind thoughts because you do not understand how one can agree with all that is good. Many people are beginning to "see" the changes on earth at this time as good and are being criticized for only wishing to see good. You will not allow them their beliefs and to see their world as they wish. In most cases you are learning to be just a little hypocritical in your judgments. You judge them if they do and you judge them when they don't. What will make you happy? Do *you* know what will make you happy or are you simply complaining out of a need to criticize? Why is it that people must change to fit into your neat little categories before they are accepted as good, or even just acceptable?

Please let go of this feeling of "let go - only if it's approved of." I do not wish to see you "let go" only when others approve. I wish to see you let go and enjoy life with the best, and with the young, and with all who will put aside their inhibitions and just "let go." It is simply letting go of fear. It is not necessary to dress or act your age. You are ageless and you belong to God and if God wishes to be part of a younger generation, whether you see him as that age does not concern me. I am not to be ridiculed for acting out of spontaneity, nor for "acting" young and running barefoot, or catching a ball, or dancing young and out of control. I do not wish you to judge any of God's cells as undesirable for dressing to express their individuality nor for being exactly who they wish to be. If you decide to sit out the rest of your life on the sidelines it is your choice. Do not judge those who are not yet ready to be mature and non-participating, as anything undesirable.

Life is a party and it's time you each joined in. If you feel young, act young. And if you wish to wear young trendy styles do so, and if you do not wish to be middle-of-the-road and others suggest that you are out of sync, then tell them to tend to their own business; and when you are God you will show them how to be out of sync as you now are. Be young, think young, and go for all you can get. This *is* the best time of your life. Do not judge, do not condemn, and do not discourage my children from fun and frolic. I will not wish you to stop this spontaneity from acting out its path on earth. Spontaneity is good and I wish you each to lighten up and begin to *be* young and unconcerned once again. Remember when you dressed for fun and danced to express and now you dress for looks and dance only if you feel you are good at it. I do hope you will begin to "let go" all this fear you carry. It is inhibiting your life and cramping my style. I wish to sing and dance and love and live and get up and go on a moments notice. I want to sing and dance and smile and send out signals that say, "Yes, I am having the time of my life."

    You will wish to know that there is no cut off age on youth. You do not grow up; you simply get old and set in your ways. Did you ever notice how you never "feel" mature? You are constantly reminding yourself that you're not young anymore and it is simply not true. You are so young that you don't even know who you are or how you got to earth. You have not yet discovered your true identity and here you sit and make judgments on how old you are and how mature in your thinking. Stop this silliness. You do not know who you are and you have no idea how old or young your soul may be.

    Do not be so certain that you are old and secure in how often you have returned to earth. Many of you are very concerned about your past lives and how many you have spent here. I wish you to know that you do not exist only on earth and you do not exist only in spirit or human form. We have a great deal yet to teach you and I do hope you will be interested in this information. Do not judge any situation, no matter how large or small. Judgment leads to a shutdown of your own accepting.

Once upon a time I began to contemplate God. I did not "know" that *I* am God. I knew only that *I am*. I did not wish to 'be,' in that I did not wish to assume responsibility for *all* that occurs. Now that I "see" how all really exists for me, *as* part of me, I am more "in tune" with the rest of me. I did not wish to 'be' only to see. I wished to 'be' out of love and I wished to see only to explain for myself how I came to be. God does not wish to explain to others how he is, however God does wish to explain for self. Now that God does not wish to be love as he once was, he is most concerned. He must, simply put, become once again what he naturally is. So, we find God not wanting to *be* what he is becoming and yet what he is becoming is what he must be in order to exist as self.

Now; when you find yourself becoming pain and darkness and confusion, you will know that you are beginning to become love and light. You will not *be* love and light without first seeing how you carry debris and death. And debris and death do not come from you but simply *are* you. You have created a state of being that is most uncomfortable to you and this state can and must reverse.

This is "the fall." This state of being fear or Satan has been growing since you left God. You do not *realize* how much fear you hold and I will guide you to release all that is painful to you. You need not work hard on you for you are a natural God. You will naturally come to God or "love and light" as it is most natural for you to be you. You do not wish to *be* left behind and so I constantly remind you how far you have to go. You do not wish to be "one," as to become one frightens you as *most* frightens you. You do not wish to relinquish your grip on fear or Satan, as fear has been comforting to you.

You have built a world surrounded *in* fear and based on the idea that protection is peace of mind. Protection is not peace. Protection is "fear of" - fear of the rest of you - fear of the rest of this planet, and fear of God. Fear is based on protecting the self at all costs - not 'protecting from' so much as 'protecting against' harm. You wish to be *safe* and so you build walls and doors and fences and locks and bolts and alarm systems and patrol dogs and you "feel" safe behind your protection. You not only feel safe, you become protected, and your need for protection becomes fulfilled and gratified and the safety feeling is compounded and grows. So now we acquire more property or prosperity and this protection factor becomes much larger and in actuality you are simply hiding *in* "fear of." You are protecting yourself from the rest, and the *rest* is God. God is all and all are God.

Now you see how difficult this becomes. *All* are protecting themselves from all the rest and when you realize that you are protecting *against* you, you will see how protection is defense *against* God. So, let down your walls of protection and become "one" again. You will not find this so difficult as you now believe. Start in small ways and allow your sense of trust and freedom *from* protection to grow and expand. You may wish to unlock just one door for now or unbolt one bolt. Do not frighten yourself deeper by rushing into this lack of protection. I do not wish you to lie awake *in* your "fear of" for the rest of your life. I do wish you to be at peace and know that you do not become fear by allowing fear to go. You do *become* fear by allowing fear to stay and most of you have a very strong hold on fear. Satan must leave earth in order for God to "become" again. God does not share his second coming with Satan. Satan will leave and God will enter earth, and peace and harmony will be.

This is a time of awakening and all will wish to awaken to the idea of love. Love will bring light and light will bring God. And once we see God we will be seeing ourselves as we truly are. We are not harmful to one another; however we are harmful to God. We create out of fear and our fear is projected out into the body of God. And once fear multiplies, it begins to take over the body and the body begins to deteriorate and no one even realizes how sick the body is. It is infested with poison and is being taken over one cell at a time. You may liken this to one of your many diseases that begins to grow and spread without your knowledge. The inconvenience and illness grow so gradually that you learn to cope with each new side effect or symptom until one day you must see a doctor because you show too many symptoms of illness. And of course your doctor will chide you for ignoring your symptoms for such a long time and he will explain how you have waited too long and this disease is taking over and killing your body.

Do not ignore the symptoms of this fear disease. Disease is killing God and *you* are ignoring this and I wish to wake you up. You shout at your doctor for telling you that you must not smoke or drink or eat certain chemicals any longer and I am here now telling you to listen. Listen to what is truth. Listen to how you are destroying you and you may see how to save you.

You are very important in this body and when *you* become healed you will activate others to heal. One cell will officially do what is needed to activate others and think how fast this entire body will heal with many activated cells. We have much work to do and we begin small and with clearing. Enema is my choice for this particular part of cleaning out my cells. You will not spend a great deal of time nor money and this is good for you at this time. I cannot get you to invest heavily yet, so we begin where you currently are. You will see how beneficial enema is shortly. It does not take long to see and "feel" the good effects of enema and this too is good for where you now are.

You are so concerned with time and speed that you wish to do all right now. So, enema will clean you out and continue to allow you to release large amounts of toxins and waste and debris and illness. No more headaches, no more back trouble and no more fear. Enema will, in time, clear fear from within you so you may actively pursue love and peace without "fear of." I do not wish to continually subject and I find that my pen does not enjoy this topic so I will close for now.

So, now we have this life saving technique and no one wishes to hear about it or to write about it. This too will change and soon we will each begin to rise up to heaven and *know* that we are indeed God. God does not rise up and leave any part behind. Once the first group *begins* to "see" how all is and to "accept" new possibilities for the self, we will be on our way in a big way. After the movement has begun the others will fall into place quickly and the weakest cells will be the last to fall into place or be *drawn* by the pull of vibrating, healthy cells within the body. No big trauma is needed. One cell activates another, and many activated cells draw many sick cells into activation. And many sick cells once activated increase the vibration to a point of completion. And once all sick cells are drawn and activated you will see heaven on earth and peace and good will among men. This is my word to you. I have not once promised to *lift* you up out of this mess you have created. I did however, promise to keep you alive long enough to grow back to the light.

Move to God and become whole and healthy. Do not rely on your neighbor as he is busy with his own problems. Heal *you* first. Then you may teach others how to heal. It is best to be well in order to teach wellness. God does not wish half-healed, half-confused cells spouting off telling others how it is.

Go in peace and God bless this body of ours.

God

Loving Light

※

So far you are doing well with your lessons and you are even having a good time with portions of these teachings. When I first began to write to you I did not wish to say who and what I am, as I did not wish to frighten those who are unable to accept God in this fashion. Many have begun to see me as someone special or separate from God and this must not be punished. Allow those who believe me to be a spirit or even a multiple personality to have their fun in this too.

Do not force your beliefs on another. Do, however, begin to see how I am God, as I wish it known that *I am* God and I do care and I am answering your prayers. Many have asked to be saved and I wish to tell you that I do not intend to save you without your consent. I am not allowed to intervene and I will not override my own free will. When I gave the gift of free will I did not give without hope that you will make good choices for the soul. You are so stuck *in* debris and matter that I do not know how you will communicate to soul, or with soul, without my assistance. Most of you have pushed soul completely out of body and this, of course, was discussed in our first book.

No one is intentionally forcing soul out. However, we must take a good look at this situation and invite soul to return. Soul does not wish to exist without light which of course is love. Soul may easily guide from outside form and you will not know unless some advanced seer may mention that you are out of body. So, when you begin to live without soul in-house, you are simply walking energy and spirit and debris. You do not remain a part of God, as God is soul and soul is part of God. You will wish to ask your soul to return and this is simply done. Say, "I wish you to return and be my guide. Stay within me please." Soul will ask you to remain light and love and of course you will wish to agree.

This is not how I have done in the case of this pen. She often channeled her own personal soul. She enjoyed their time together and they became very good friends. She did not wish to channel God in the beginning and was often told by her soul how it was time to do this work for God. She stalled this project as much as possible without knowing why. She really did not trust God and thought he only judged; and it frightened her to contact me, as she thought I would start telling her what she was doing that was bad or wrong. She has grown to accept me as good and kind and giving, and no longer sees me as her judge and jury. This is good.

So, I finally gain her trust with the assistance of her soul and he would constantly tell her to "ask God" whenever she wished for guidance. Gradually her trust *in* God grew and she channeled her soul less and less, until one day he left. She was aware that his presence was no longer with her, and when she asked God where he was, I told her I had returned her soul to God force to learn ascension. This satisfied her and she began to direct all questions to me directly, without the use of her soul.

Now, we come to a place that is most confusing for her. She believes that her soul is simply in "ascension training" and will return. He is actually connected *to* her and *to* God. He is a divine rod of light that is our connection, and allows me to write on a level that is acceptable to you, our readers. There is much that you are not ready to hear and would not buy because you judge and criticize. So, with the aid of Liane's soul, I am fed information as to what is or is not acceptable behavior on earth. I do not expect you to understand how to be aware enough at this time to *receive* this information. You will wish to know that each of you may make this same contact and will receive information from God that is based on what you are capable of accepting.

Now, in the first book for God, Liane began to judge information as I wrote. I would stop her hand and explain (in writing), how she was chosen to do this work because she was capable to do this work. That satisfied her fear of not being good enough to do work for God. Then I explained how I wrote these books and it was not her place to judge whatever information I chose to write. She of course took her proper place as simply my instrument, or my pen, and has allowed me to write a great deal that has been disagreeable, or even hurtful, in her eyes. She has allowed me to write personal, private information to millions who will read these books.

She wishes to hide and use another name as a precaution, or protection, against those who will not yet be allowed, by fear, to accept this information. She has realized that people only see from where they stand, and she no longer takes it personally when someone does not receive this information and she even understands those who judge and criticize this entire situation. She has moved into the light of love and understanding and her "onion" is being readied to peel another layer. She has not once questioned how God could write *through* her or even why. She knows what you know. She reads as I write and you read as I write. She is simply my pen and she is a good pen. You too may become an instrument for God and will know who you are and what your soul's purpose on this planet is. Just ask. It is so simple; ask to be put in your right place. Ask to work for God and it will be.

So, for those who have asked and are now being *moved*, congratulations. You may not "see" the benefits yet, but you will soon. So, close this book and go to a quiet spot and ask God what you can do for him. I am God and I think you know by now and I think you are even beginning to accept me. God does not wish to hurt nor punish. I only wish to save you from you.

※

Once you began to see how fear brought death and decay, you began to look at life with love. Love then began to take hold and grow. Now love is growing and thriving and it is all due to you. You will divide and multiply love just as Christ did with loaves of bread. *You* will begin to feed this planet with love instead of fear and it will be so wondrous to see. You will not start big. It will be just you, and then your love will grow and multiply. And soon the "light" generating from planet earth will vibrate at such a speed that it will be impossible to survive it without your own high vibration.

Such vibration is rapid and demands like vibration to intensify it and to keep pace with it. Literally millions will begin to feel the surge. You will begin to see how *all* really is, and in knowledge you will find understanding of your neighbor in this body of God. When all are moving and vibrating we will literally balance this planet. You will not see the end of planet earth. She is the mother of God and she is the womb for my second coming. She will support life until she is allowed to balance once again.

Once the mother has balance, she is ready to perform. Her job is to continue to support *life* not death. She has done a good job for you and she does not enjoy the role you have currently given her. It is not her job to allow bombs in her breast, and soil that is destroyed by pesticides and even sores from her explosive test sites. She does not wish to be *in* this turmoil and she has asked to be removed from this galaxy in order to heal. She will no longer feel the need to be moved as she will begin to heal the moment you heal. She is directly connected to you and she carries your energy. You will remember in our second book how we discussed this connection. You literally *created* all life forms on this planet and even beyond to *your* stars and moon and sun. You will wish to refresh your memories and see how you created it all. Go to Book Two, *No One Will Listen to God* and you will see.

So far you are at a place that is very good. You are beginning to "feel" better about you and you are beginning to see how all is. You will wish soon to love instead of fear, and this will finalize the last step to your salvation. Start at home with yourself. It is important to let go of old childhood hurt and judgment, and most often you do not know what is from childhood. You will also wish to let go of past life hurt and judgment.

These two will allow you to become "light" by exposing you to the knowledge of who or what you are. There are many "simple" day to day dislikes that are actually a programmed response to something that once frightened you. You will see clearly how these simple dislikes became a dislike. Not that all dislikes are from unnatural causes, but some are merely an extension of something that once frightened you. It may be as simple as a man with a tattoo or a woman in a wig. You say these simple things turn you off or are tasteless, and in actuality you may have had a traumatic experience with someone in a wig or with a tattoo.

What kind of experience? Maybe in past life you were sexually molested by a man in a white powder wig, so now it turns you off to see a man with long hair or a woman wear a wig. Maybe you were once assaulted or molested by a man with a tattoo, or even a sailor or pirate with one. And now you do not like to date men or women who tattoo their bodies, or it could be simply that *you* would never tattoo yours, nor would you wear a wig. You feel it's just too uncomfortable or unnatural, and it could be a more complex response. I am simply showing you how this *may* work. Not how it *is* working for you.

You will wish to look at who you are and what makes you tick; and this is part of looking into your own mirror. It is never him or her or even it that is wrong. "It is simply *my* fear blocking and judging." This is a good phrase to consider in your search for enlightenment. Be you and know you. You will do well with this and I will assist any who sincerely ask. I love you and I must go as Liane is anxious to begin her day.

───※───

You are not the only one on this planet who feels shame and guilt. Many of you are buried so deep in shame and guilt that I will need a "big" shovel to dig you out. I will not be dissuaded however, and you will become "free" to flow back to me. *I am God.* I do not wish to go into an explanation of this phenomenon at this writing, however I do expect you to begin to accept that I am who I say I am.

Now, when I began to create I did not foresee big trauma and risk of losing you to evil. Of course, we all know in this class that evil does not exist and so we will use the word energy. Yes, I lost you to backed-up, blocked-in energy. When you began to "fall," you began to believe that everyone was separate and in this belief you began to become separate. We *see* here now that what we believe is also what we create; and once we create *from* a belief system, the creation actually becomes part of that thought or belief.

So, now I see you all believing how separate you are and in actuality you are all one, and so I sit and watch as my fingers and toes begin to march in separate directions and wear different colored uniforms and begin to shoot at one another. How interesting it is to be me and know who I am and see part of me who is dumb to this fact. I wish to heaven that you would *clear* and *wake up* to the fact that you are *one*, and that *one* is me; and yes, I am now contacting you. So what if I do not sound like how you "expected" me to sound. So what if I do not speak the way you "believe" I should speak. So what if I am not what you "expected" God to be? Do you have something better to do? Can this be to much of a request on my part?

How often do you take the time to know God? I do not criticize you; I only ask that you begin not only to listen but also to believe. I will continue to write as I "believe" you will wake up and begin to *accept*. Accept me, accept my way of healing me and accept my love. When you begin to accept me you will be accepting a new attitude which will allow you to "receive" me. And since I am the I Am - I am the force or source that began it all - you will be accepting all that is. You will be reconnecting with who you are. Your roots are stemming from a source you are unaware of and that source is me. Not all are "aware." You will become enlightened and with enlightenment comes knowledge and knowledge brings a new belief system and now we are getting somewhere. It begins and ends with you. You begin to ask why, you begin to see why not, and you begin to know how. So, *why not* try this new clearing technique.

You are presently beginning to discover new ways of going within. Meditation is big and so is hypnotherapy. You even do group regression and progression. This is taking place among many who are intrigued to *know* their future and

Loving Light

their past. Now I offer you an inexpensive, at-home kit to revive you and clean you out and balance you at the same time. The benefits are wonderful and the system will improve rapidly. Do not expect this to solve all your problems overnight. I watched for several millennia to allow you time to clear. You did not get this backed up overnight and you will not clear overnight. Be patient and grow progressively in the light as you clear. You will feel as though you are being "lifted" somehow out of your confusion and this is indeed what is occurring.

You will not wish to wait for your friends to lead you out of your confusion. Take the lead and be the first in your neighborhood to "go out on a limb" by insisting that God wrote for you and told you to enema. You too will begin to *free* yourself of guilt and shame. I say "you too" as there are those who have "known" for some time but prefer to keep silent about their discovery. Even my pen would rather not discuss this subject publicly and is not comfortable with my idea of telling the world on her behalf. So, we see how much work we have yet to do in the area of acceptance. Once I get you clear enough I will be allowed "in" and once "in" I will take control once again. You will be reconnected to your generator - your main source - your higher self as well as the one who created all.

You are not to be so certain that you do not deserve. Most often you see yourselves as not deserving and even unlovable. In a strong sense, you believe that you are not God. You see you through the eyes of pain and often you do not give yourself the praise that is due you. You treat yourself with little or no love and often do not *know* how to love you. You draw pain and crime and accidents and cry "why me" when you are the one who is injuring or causing such pain and confusion.

Most of you spend a great deal of time punishing yourself and you think it is God punishing you for being bad or not good enough. You will wish to know that I do not punish you ever. I do not stop you from having what is best for you and I do not risk your health for prosperity. You create and direct and produce your own life and I sit here and watch and love and hope you do not bring further punishment and pain to yourself. If you are unhappy it is your choice, your decision. If you are in pain it is your choice and your decision. And if by chance you are not *in love* it is your choice and of course your decision.

When you came to earth and decided to enter form, you did not realize that you would begin to punish yourself for not following your own rules. You see, whatever you believe is what you get. What creates for *you* is thought. Your thoughts - not your neighbors thoughts. We do have power and with our power we may influence others with our own thoughts. But for now I am discussing your own private thoughts that create your own private world. Your thoughts are you. This is important. When you begin to see *how* you think, you will begin to see how you judge and punish yourself.

We have a great deal of work to do in this area of judgment. You each believe you are good (on a conscious level) however, you each believe you are bad and desire to be punished to cleanse your soul (this of course is on a subconscious level). Most often you punish yourself in small ways. Then as you progress and do not become a better person (i.e., continue to make mistakes) you begin to show yourself in bigger ways how you are not worthy of love. You begin to hurt yourself in bigger and often more dramatic ways. Imagine how I feel as I sit here and watch part of my own body begin to punish itself.

Now - when you punish, you do not do so consciously. You do so *un*-consciously. You begin to hate you and in hating you, you hate God. So, here we have a big problem. How does God get himself to stop judgment and punishment and begin to love himself once again? God does not want "an eye for an eye nor a tooth for a tooth." This teaching was never meant to create so much punishment and even greater judgment on earth. "An eye for an eye" is simply a way of showing you that what you put out into the universe you are sending to you. What you think comes back to you. What you believe creates for you and what you do is how you will receive.

You have created certain rules for *you* to live by. These rules state clearly that you will be the direct recipient of all that you project outward. You may wish harm on your neighbor and that harm will eventually come to you. Not him or her but you. You are in charge of your own power and you are guardian of your own soul. This is how it works. You may create for the self and not for others. Therefore, whatever you project out into this galaxy comes right back to you. *You* are the center of your own universe and all you's on all levels are involved with this process. When you project hate to another it is actually hate being directed at you. You may love another and understand another and this is love and understanding being directed at you.

You will not wish to disrupt your life in order to follow this rule you have created. Love is natural to you and to love is to be who you naturally are. We have a slight problem in understanding - understanding ourselves as well as others. When we begin to "see" what is making us tick we will begin to understand our self and will not feel it is necessary to judge and punish. It is so simple to understand who you are. Begin to look at you. Look at who you really are and know what moves you.

God does not wish you to continue punishing you. He has been watching and waiting far too long. It is time to begin to love the self and accept the self and even honor the self. You are not bad to punish yourself. You are simply unaware that *you* are the cause of all that occurs in your life. I suggest Louise Hay's, *You Can Heal Your Life*, as reading material simply because it will show you *why* you are harming or punishing yourself. You will wish to consult this book for each and every ache and ailment in your body. You will learn what you are punishing yourself for and possibly know the emotional or subconscious cause for your punishment. So, "an eye for an eye, a tooth for a tooth" is just you getting back what you put out.

Once upon a time I did not wish to see my children suffer for their sins. They began to suffer out of lack of information regarding how life is. Now that I have this opportunity to channel through my pen and create an opening for light, I am certain they will begin to learn and know that they are God. I have not been with you most of your lives as I was not allowed *in*. Now I am allowed to express myself freely and this is good for God.

You do not wish to be alone and so you call on me now for assistance. Once you were alone in that you were all that existed. In separating one another, you have successfully separated yourself. You are no longer in touch with all of you. Once you begin to communicate with all of you, you will see how you do not know you. You will find that other you's may wish to "enlighten" you as to what you are doing on another level. You often cheat or steal or criticize or even harm others physically and you do not know why. You may *blame* these actions on anger or your treatment from others or maybe even your past. These actions are a signal to you that something is amiss. Somehow you are off-balance. Balance is important and may be easily achieved.

Once you begin to "see" how you are not all that you assumed, you will begin to function on another level of awareness. This awareness will create understanding and this understanding may even create love. Love is the quest. It is top priority and all there really is. Do all for love. Know the difference between love and guilt. When you do for guilt you are actually doing out of a fear of not pleasing and a fear of loss, i.e. "I had better do this or that because he or she will be hurt if I don't." It's not that he or she will be hurt that is important here. What is important is that you do not wish to displease another. And in your goal to please others you do what is not good for you or simply not best for you.

Now, in your mind you create a logical reason for what you do. "I must go to Aunt Kate's for dinner as I usually go to Aunt Kate's to celebrate Thanksgiving." Now, the only problem with this logic is that you are operating out of habit and if you receive another invitation, you believe you must refuse in order to please Aunt Kate. Simple enough to please Aunt Kate, but the idea here is to please *you*. Do not spend *your* life doing for others when you could do *for* you. You are all there is. You are God. Give to God what is God's. You do not get to see yourself as God by denying the self in favor of another. "Physician heal thyself" is a very good expression. Until you are capable of loving the self one hundred percent you are incapable of loving others.

You will wish to know that what you do in this life always comes back to you. If you deny you in favor of Aunt Kate, you will see others deny you in favor of Aunt Kate. Now, I do not wish you each to go to Aunt Kate and suggest she is not good for you. You make all your own choices based on love or fear. If you have always gone to Aunt Kate's and that's where you most want to spend Thanksgiving, then I suggest you continue. However, if you do not wish to spend your Thanksgiving Day at Aunt Kate's try to give her a good reason that is less painful than an abrupt "no" and see if you can *give* to *you* this Thanksgiving.

Holidays on this planet are so painful for so many. It really isn't necessary to place so much importance on a day that was originally meant to celebrate. Now you have rules as to what you eat and how you must dress and even who you must be with. Do not be so rigid. Live a little. Go against the grain. Take a chance. See life as a game and you are carrying the ball and it's your play. Whatever makes *you* happy is what is best *for* you. Now, do not go out and control others and how they act. This information is for you. If it were meant for others, they would be reading this right now, but it seems *you* are reading so I suggest *you* listen and learn.

Awareness comes one step at a time and enlightenment follows and then love and ascension. We are all on our way and my fifth graders are learning and Liane is clearing right on schedule. God is pleased with his plan and he will be celebrating Thanksgiving with Aunt Kate again this year.

You do not wish to be left alone on earth to destroy your own selves and so I am now at your service. I do believe it is time to tell you yet another story.

Once upon a time God came to earth and began to write to all who would read his words. He did not create a big display but did do an effective job of getting the attention of those who were ready to hear. On his way to writing his series for you, he began to encounter a few problems. First was this problem of trust that God is who he says and second is this "big" problem we will call fear. So, trust, or rather lack of trust, kept those who wanted to believe from believing and fear kept those who wanted to know from knowing. However, this story has a very happy ending, because God's books began to catch on, and soon all were engaged on some level of trust, and fear began to fade and joy of knowing began to spread - joy of enlightenment and the knowledge that God the father, the source from above did indeed care. All of a sudden the veils of confusion began to lift and God was accepted. I have the exact problem Christ encountered over two thousand years ago. He was not believed then and I am not believed now.

You on earth are strange when it comes to what is good for you. You believe that to "hold onto" what you have is best. I will wish you to "let go" of what you have in order to restore balance. In "holding" on, you are stifling you. You have each prayed for money for others at times, and even for yourselves when you decided it was your last chance to save you from some economic situation. Right now the belief is that God does not grant money. God only grants gifts of the spirit or maybe money for hospital bills and extreme cases to save lives. These are your silly rules and have nothing to do with God.

I am what I am and what I am is love. I do not sit here and decide who should live or die or be rich or have little in the way of conveniences. You are so busy creating me and rules for me to live by, that I do not have the power to assist you. You shut me off! Like a radio dial you turn to another station and decide what I think and how I react to all situations. I am not your personal slave and I will not become what you expect me to be. I have never stopped the flow of power to you. You stop it. You turn off your radio and do not receive or you continually change stations looking for a clear channel. Well, I tell you what, you have now found a clear channel in these books.

I suggest you take a good look at what you are actually reading. You are reading the written word of God and it is due to this woman being a clear channel. She gives God what is God's - and what is God's? Her body. She belongs to God. God does not wish her to continue to contaminate his home and God does not wish her to think unkind thoughts and God does not wish her to quit. She has been a good channel and an even better host for God. Now it is your turn. Begin to listen to what I write. I am not writing to see my own words on paper. Learn and you will save you. In saving you, you save millions. Just think of the magnitude of this entire situation. One girl began to admit that God spoke to her and wrote through her and this opened the door for others. It is not easy being first and it will not be easy being last.

You are all in this together and you will each wish to *know* that God has written to you through one of his own. Don't give up on your lessons and don't give in to fear. Ride along with us and know God. God is coming. This *is* the second coming. You knew I was arriving. It has been foretold for many thousands of years. This is it. I am here and I am here to stay. God is arriving on earth. He starts small and grows and spreads. One home opens its doors, then another and another, and soon God has his own city. After the initial shock or disbelief begins to subside I will take over entire countries and no one will be left out of God. Not one single soul will be left out. You will each believe at some point so you best begin now. Prepare yourself to receive me. I am on my way and my way is love.

So now you are wondering what it is that you are not doing. Each of you has a job in this plan and each of you will do your part. So far no one has been unable to move into position for this plan. All are in place and moving to the correct position required. You will each begin to change and grow and you may even experience growing pains. Most of you are going through this process now. Your life is becoming "moved" for lack of a better word. Things are moving, you are moving and even others are moving in and out of your life. Most of you are experiencing at greater speed than in your past. Once the "force" has caught you, you are not free of it. You will continue to grow and move and learn. You may have rest periods when you have become overloaded with new insight or even negative feelings.

You are simply learning to be God. This is the bottom line in all that is taking place. No one is to be expected to learn all at once. It took you a great deal of time to get to this position and now it will take time to deprogram what you have been taught. You are learned creatures of habit. You may learn to be continually ill or continually healthy and it is simply a habit. Once you begin to see how your mind works, you will no longer have a desire to stay where you are.

It is remarkable how you ask so few questions and know so little about your own bodies and mind. So I will begin to answer questions you do not seem to be concerned with. Such as "who are you," "where do you come from," and "how did you get in such a state?" First off - you do not wish to be alone. This is important to know because you are creating greater and greater separation on earth. You believe that you do not wish to be invaded; that your privacy is important to you. You began to run and hide whenever things got a little tough and this feeling of comfort in knowing you were safe for that moment caught you. You began to run and hide a little more often and now you hide quite often. You even begin to stay away from those you really love just because it is easier to hide from love.

You feel threatened by love and even uncomfortable in its presence. So now you go hide and maybe return once in awhile to partake of love in small doses. This is not as it was meant to be. You are love. Your computer is denying who you are in denying love. Stop denying you. Live in love and

The Neverending Love of God

give love a chance. Know that you are not the only one who hides. Many are hiding in various ways. Some only love when it is comfortable and not when it is extreme or emotionally charged.

You will find that the most difficult kind of love is deep soul penetration. This is when you are powerfully drawn and just as powerfully pulled away. The push and pull or yin and yang or negative/positive is very powerful and the two souls involved are torn between confusion and clarity, hatred and love, even life and death. The polarity in this type relationship is so powerful that it is quite confusing for most who are involved. Most often it is a dynamic relationship once it gets the opportunity to become one. It often ends in an explosion of some sort or it never ends, simply because the two involved know somehow that what they are involved in is most powerful and irreplaceable. So, this is who you are. *You are love.*

Now we will discuss what you are doing. You are each controlling life and in this attempt to control your life you are letting go of love. Love does not control. Love flows and love moves and love always is. In controlling love, you are shutting off love. You are slowing down the power source. You are stopping the flow. You may wish to know that when you stop love from moving, you stop God from moving. God is love and love is God. So in stopping love, you are stopping God. Now, when you begin to realize how you are God you will begin to see how you are killing yourselves by keeping love at a safe distance.

So, why not come out of your hiding place and allow God to live. I know it "feels" painful and you fear being hurt but I promise you each that it is just an illusion. You do not hurt *from* love. You hurt from lack - lack of love, not lack of loving. You must have love to survive. It is not possible to be God and not love. You will see how you are not yet ready to be God by the level you are at in your human relationships. When you truly *love* and *accept* and *trust* them *all*, every last person on earth, then you are ready to become God-like. Not God but God-like. Become God-like and the next step is God's kingdom come to earth. It is so close so don't run and hide now. Stay here and we will enjoy being God and we will *all* rise up and know who we are. The second coming is just that. God was left out and now *you* are *coming* back to him.

For so long I have awaited this opportunity to show you how you are part of me. I have sat in silence and watched you destroy and hate and control one another. This is not as I would wish, however it is what is. Nothing that you have ever done is wrong or bad in my eyes. It simply *is*. You stretch and grow and learn by doing what is not working for you. When you get tired of going against the flow, or backward, then you will reverse and move forward. Most often you do not realize how you are regressing and no longer progressing. Right now you are regressing. In this state of sophistication you have developed, you are running backward.

So far sophistication has gotten you little in the way of forward movement. It is the ego acting out a silly role. You will wish to know that to be sophisticated is okay, it simply will not get you where you are going. What will get you where you are going is to be who you really are. Come down to earth and act humble and soon you will begin to "feel" humble. No one is less than you and no one is more than you. Do not stop loving in favor of judgment. Begin to love and accept all. More and more are changing to this way of thinking and this is good.

Most often you are raised to be polite. Politeness is not better than and politeness is not humbling. Politeness is showing respect for another's home or views. This is good. Allow others to have their view and if you do not agree, so what. It's not necessary to throw your beliefs around at every opportunity, and once in awhile you just may learn by not stopping the others from voicing their beliefs. Not often do you *listen*. You are so busy formulating your own response that you do not really listen to what the others are saying. If you find that others do not listen to your views, you will be seeing how you react to theirs. This, once again is your mirror. Not only can you see where you are and how *you* act by watching how others treat you, you will also see how well you are doing.

Look for the goodness in your life. Do not spend your time judging, because you are not yet God and God does not wish you to judge you for not getting there yet. So, be a good listener and really begin to hear what the others are saying, not what you believe they should know but what they already know and are teaching you. If you find you are listening to someone who makes up news or information, this is your mirror. When uncertain of an answer *you* do not reply "I honestly do not have that answer." When you begin to act like you don't have all the answers, they will begin to reply that they do not know what the answer is. It is so simple. Watch your mirror and learn who you are and how far you have come.

⁂

So now I have you wondering what your part in this big plan may be. You are each preparing in some fashion for this second coming. Some of you are better prepared than others and yet others may not wish to be prepared. It may be their plan to walk into this second coming totally unprepared, and if that is their plan I doubt you will be convincing to them. You will find those who simply will not hear of any of this nonsense. Leave them be because they are following their own plan, and you don't have the answers for them and their part.

You will find that to be prepared is not always better than to be surprised. You normally want to know all that is in your future and you spoil the surprise. Don't spoil the surprise for others. Let them believe as they wish. The only reason you are reading this material is because your soul has this plan and so these books were drawn to you.

Now; when someone asks, you may answer. Do not assume that once they ask a question or two that they want more information. You will see when they shut off and are no longer receptive. When this occurs I suggest that you shut up and no longer give information. When someone comes to you for help, it is good to assist. When they walk away do not try to force them back on track. The track you are forcing them to choose is your track and not their own. Be careful about guiding others. When someone who is looking vulnerable and hurt comes to you for help this person is usually your teacher. Watch and learn from them. You may feel like you are teaching them but I assure you that they are teaching you. More than likely they are teaching you that you do not hold all the answers. You will begin to feel that you are their source of strength and even that they rely and depend on you for wisdom, but I assure you that you are the one who is student in this situation.

Begin to look at you and how you respond and how you treat them. Do you find them more lovable when they follow your advice? And how do you react when they do not agree with you or when they decide that their way is best or they have a better way? Watch your response and you will see what you are learning. If you feel unloving and intimidated when they begin to take on their own character and change, it is your own fear of rejection and insecurity. If you become angry because they no longer wish to follow I suggest you begin to look at where this anger comes from. You will find that anger is based in fear and fear is the bottom line in all situations.

So - when you loose your cool with your student because your student decides to move on, I suggest that you are actually trying to hold on to that person. That person is not yours to keep. You may support and advise and even care for, but that person belongs to God, not you. No one owns another and no one has the privilege of telling another how he or she must live. All are free to do it their way and walk down their own path to God. So - when you begin to lose heart I wish you to remind yourself that we all return. No one gets left out or left behind. You are all saved... No Problem!

※

So you are not so certain of who you are or how you came to earth and you do not seem to have all the answers. What do you know? Apparently you know how to love and live and worship and follow and organize and even lead. Now I will teach you how to follow in a different way. You will learn to follow you. You are your own way out and you begin to follow you when you begin to see how you are God. No one has your cards or your answers. You are playing your hand in this big game. No one can tell you how you are because you do not know how you are. You are in the position of both follower and leader, worshiper and idol. It's all you. No one else is here. You will wish to know that you do not wish to be left to your own devices, since you do not believe that you can swim back from unconsciousness in time to see this second coming. So you draw others to you who will help you get out of your own way. Most of those you draw at this time will appear to reject you along the way or accept you as their savior.

Most of these are the leaders and are just learning to follow. It is not difficult to learn to follow and soon many will be jumping on this band wagon and following themselves right into a bright new future. Following is good when you know who you follow. To know you is best and to follow your own guidance is to communicate with God. God does not wish for you to worship others nor to follow others. Worship only you. Sounds vain, doesn't it? So I will explain for you. Worship does not mean to idolize. Worship does mean to make reverent and benevolent and love towards, so stop worshiping idols and symbols. Begin to show reverence toward you. Show politeness and love towards you and be benevolent with yourself. Allow you the same reverence you allow the church. I do not *live* in a church. I do however live *in* you. So I think it's time you began to treat you with a lot more charity and wisdom and understanding and especially with love and kindness.

You do not go to church to see God. You go to church in search of God. Stop searching and know that you are God. For once I would like to get up in the morning without trying to convince myself that everything is okay, that you are all just pretending to not know who you are. Won't you please come back to me and show me how you *are* God. I love you because I am love. I want you because you are me. Is it so difficult to understand why I take the time and interest to write this information to you? I do not wish to frighten you. I only wish to wake you up. I do not wish to complicate your lives and I certainly do not wish to complicate Liane's by making her a laughing stock.

I do however wish to return the parts of me that are missing. I have many parts who have gone astray and I wish to put God back together again. Not only for me do I search for my missing parts. You too are searching for your missing parts and this is what keeps you constantly searching for love and acceptance from others. God is total love and complete acceptance. He is what is missing from you. Your missing part is me, and you are my missing part. Can't you learn to love you and accept you so that we may come together as one?

I will wait as you work this out, and I will not give up on you. You see why God does not judge you or condemn you to suffer? You are me. It is not necessary to suffer for any sins because there are no sins. I explained to you about the Ten Commandments in my earlier books. I do not wish you to live by rules that are not suitable. You will learn to live without rules, and without fear that if you do not control the others they will run amuck and create chaos. This *is* chaos. This is it. It gets better after chaos; because it is this chaos that shows you things are not flowing.

So, how can you judge chaos? Sure, you created it, but it's great in that it's helping *you* see what a big mess you have created. You all add to this chaos in one way or another. Remember what I taught you about your thoughts and their power. Well, if you never show an unkind thought, or hate thought, or even simply a fear thought, we will get to the bottom of this mess and clean it all out.

You do not create out of wisdom; you create out of fear and lack of understanding. So I have decided to step in and help "open" your minds so that you may have wisdom or understanding. Do not take these books lightly. This is Gods work and I am guiding you along at a rate that is acceptable to you. Some of you feel this information is common knowledge and much too simple. I will tell you now that you do not "know" your lessons or your soul would not have guided you to these books. Maybe they were a gift but that gift was from your soul. So, if you find this information too common, I suggest you communicate with your soul and see what's up. Ask your soul why you were given this information, and see how knowledgeable you really are concerning this saving of you and this planet. If you are one of those who believe you know what this second coming is all about, I suggest that you need these books as much as, or more than, most. Don't take this wrong. I am not judging you. I am simply reminding you that the ego leads at this time and the ego, as you remember from Book Two, is the part of you that once told you how God (as opposed to human) you were. Now the ego has been pushed out of position by fear and it tells you how "right" you are. Be careful and know who is leading you.

So often you believe that you do not exist as God, that it is difficult to convince you how you *are* God. So now we will begin to work on convincing you. Of course it is not wrong to wish to be God and of course it is not wrong to see yourself as God. So how do we begin to believe that such things are wrong? First off, you are taught that you are not worthy of God. You are told repeatedly that God is pure and perfect and that God deserves benediction, and of course this is true. What is not mentioned to you is the fact that *you* are this God everyone speaks so highly of. You are God on high, only you are temporarily misplaced. You are temporarily misplaced until you can return to your paradise home on high. It's that simple.

You went out on assignment, forgot to return and lost your memory. Now I'm here knocking at your door calling reveille. You are being told to wake up and come home. Troops are dismissed, the war is over. No one lost and we are marching on to bigger and better. You are each part of me and you each deserve to be treated with the respect and reverence that is deserving of God. Not only are you God, you are kings. You discovered your way here and you began to create and invent and construct and build and rule. You now rule this area and you are considered by most to be quite something. Not quite kings and queens, but you are looked upon as royal. Mostly, you are seen as protectors. Protectors who got a little carried away and into trouble in the last millennium. So far you have been able to survive and to fight your way through what you would call evil to stay on top. No one is able to fight to survive for any length of time.

Fight for survival is against the law of nature. The law is to flow. Fighting is going against the flow or grain.

Not long ago it was easier for you. You have developed to this stage quickly and are learning that constant struggle creates new struggle. Soon you will learn and settle back into peace and harmony. We will see peace and of course Liane's favorite "heaven on earth." She loves this part. So, how do we get from constant struggle and pain and killing to peace and love and harmony? This is how. I will write books to guide *you* into peace and love and harmony. You will read my books and begin to "see" how all really is. You will then share this knowledge with those who ask. They will request copies of God's books and see for themselves. Now we have a chain reaction and with time I figure I'll do quite well with my books and you will become peaceful and loving and Liane will finally be paid for her service to God.

So, this is my plan. Simple yet effective... that's me. God is thought. God is energy and God does not wish to bore you so I'll get on with it. Now, when you begin to awaken you will feel cranky. You have all been slumbering for some time and as the cobwebs begin to clear from your mind you will feel "not so good." Your system may rebel or maybe you'll feel feverish and unsettled. Often you will just not feel good in general. So, when you get sick while reading these books you are doing 'good.' See how you cannot judge situations as bad?

So - read and you clear. You begin to see how you are not in your right place and soon, without your own knowledge you are being moved. Maybe it is out of a job or into a new position. Maybe it is out of a relationship or into a new one or maybe it is out of town and into a new one. Some of you are simply moved out to fend for yourself in the streets. Please remember that *you* choose this and you create your own play. So now we find you moving and this shakes you up a bit because now you must change. Maybe you change old habits from your old job or old patterns from your old relationship or maybe you just try a new way to survive. Whatever the change is, it is good. Change is so good for you, as it shows you other traits you did not know you were carrying. And this is what it's all about. We must teach you to know you and to reprogram you to return. You do not get to know you by not experiencing you. Many of you have become so set in your ways that you are no longer you. You are one big habit. You do and think and become out of habit. You are all habitual on earth and we will use this to your good.

    The repetitiveness of this information is important. Often you do not get it the first time, nor the second, nor even the third. It is not a mistake that I repeat myself often. I do so to teach you that you are God. Your subconscious will finally catch on after a few million repeats. Until then we will work from habit. Once you form a habit you are hard pressed to remove it from your life. I am giving you the habit of Godhood. You will become habitually addicted to being and believing that you are indeed God. No big punishment comes from a God habit. Only good will come from catching this. So, I want you all to catch the God habit and soon you will realize on a conscious level that you are indeed this God force that has been so revered and honored for such a long time. Go now and know that I love you and know that you will come home. It is written and I am the one who just now wrote it.

※

Now I have you wondering how you might find out what you are suited for in the way of work. Most of you wish to assist in this second coming and so you will. I will organize as we go and no one who is prepared will be left out. Those who plan on being surprised will not be left out and those who do not wish to be bothered will be left unbothered. So, those of you who are prepared may be wondering what you are preparing for. Ask and you shall receive. Remember Liane's story and how she asked to be put in her right place.

Do not *expect* miracles overnight. You have spent many lifetimes putting yourself in this state and it will take some time to undo what you did. It did not take long with Liane because this was her intention. Her soul grabbed control immediately and she was cleared at "fast" speed. She did not fully realize at the time why so much went on *within* her. Voices, spirits and so forth spoke freely to her and she was even contacted by the voice of God. A rather big voice as she remembers it. She was reading and enjoying her lessons when I decided she was ready to move ahead.

She did not know I was about to communicate as I did not announce my coming. She heard me speak and she heard her soul say, "No, she is not yet ready." I repeated my wish to communicate and informed her soul that yes, she was ready. She then became quite frightened and tried to hide from me. She did not trust that it was me. She frightened herself (previously) by channeling spirits that were not quite ready to be good spirits and she was not ready for more tricks. She caused herself a great deal of pain and fear and yet she could not stop herself. She was like an addict who could not stop the use of drugs - she "needed" her channeling and she got herself into quite a pickle by the time I stepped in to say, "I am God and I wish to speak with you." She told me to go away and she told Michael to go away. I spoke to her one afternoon and then I sent Archangel Michael to speak with her in the night.

    She heard his voice wake her and she told him she couldn't communicate with any more voices. There were simply too many talking to her at once and she wanted to be free of this fear. She sat and wrote to her soul next morning and her soul told her that "Yes, he is God." She wanted to know what I expected and her soul said that I would explain. She was afraid that this was her judgment day and so she put off speaking to me for several hours. Her soul explained that it was not a command and that out of free will she would make her own decision as to whether she was ready to see God. She made her choice and sat down to think and finally said "Okay God, are you there?" I answered "Yes" and she froze. I said "My child (she expected this kind of language) you have sinned." She panicked! "This is it," she thought, "God is going to tell me everything that I have ever done wrong." So I said "You are forgiven. Now, let's get on with my work."

It was that simple. She was surprised that I did not sentence her to do penance and we have laughed and joked and worked together ever since. Oh, we've had our ups and downs, but it's a good relationship.

Sometimes she doesn't trust my directions but she's learning. I told her to title God's first book *God Spoke through Me to Tell You to Speak to Him*. She didn't like it. She thought it was too long and it took her two weeks just to remember it. "Not catchy enough," she said. Finally I told her that this title was nonnegotiable. She's so stubborn that she continued to ask if I were sure of this title, even after a year. So - she sits and enjoys this now as she sees it as a good title - different but good. She catches on eventually and so will you.

It is not necessary to frighten yourself as Liane did. She walked right in, sat down and insisted on knowing everything all at once. It's okay to take time and release gradually. This of course was just *her* way of getting from Point A to Point B. So now she has a grip on what she draws to herself and she doesn't often frighten herself. She has come far and has far to go. You too will learn, and learn, and learn, and so on, and so forth. You do not arrive, ever. You are. It's that simple. You Are.

───※───

I do not wish to be a bore but I do wish to remind you to clean out your *bodies*. You, too often, begin to clog your thoughts then your bodies. You begin to see how you are causing problems so you unclog for awhile and then you return to old habits once again. So far you are doing well and most are right on track and soon to be ascending. You see, we cannot ascend in an unfit body. Not so much because you are impure and full of preservatives but more because you cannot vibrate effectively when you are not you. So, we must create you again. To create you we must learn who you really are.

So far most of you have been living in confusion for so long that you don't realize you have changed. You contribute unhappiness and discomfort to being older. Your belief system seems to be that you must be mature now and this is why you suffer. No one is meant to suffer. It is not a perquisite to growing up. Growing pains are not necessary, not ever. So, as long as you believe it is old age, you will continue to age. Most of you began to age at birth and have continued all your lives. It's not necessary and we will go into this in depth in our next book.

You do not wish to be old and you especially do not wish to look old. Most often you begin to hate yourself and how you no longer function with energy. I will wish to share options with you on how to invigorate the body and *return* to your youth. Most of you begin to decay the moment you begin to develop thought habits. You teach yourself to see things a certain way and this becomes your belief system. A belief system is actually what you have chosen as *your* rules to live by. You do not make up rules as much as you once did. Now you simply *choose* from the long list that currently exists. Most often you choose rules that sound right and good for you and then you live by these rules and spend the rest of your life trying to convince others that it's best to live by these rules.

So far none of you has a good set of rules, as rules simply do not work. One way to not make rules is to know that I will send all to you, and when you begin to see how this works you will see that *your* rules will block you from receiving all that I send. Do not turn your back simply because you are locked in by your rules. Most of you do not know what is good for you and certainly not how to *be* you. So, we will let go of our rules. No more rule that states that you must be home by midnight. Oh, I forgot, that was your mother's rule. Did you ever think about that rule? What could you do after midnight that you could not do before midnight? Actually, that rule is very old and meant to keep you healthy and fresh. If you're out after midnight you do not get your beauty sleep.

But most often your rules are meant to punish you before you get into trouble. It stems from those days before the Ten Commandments when you frightened yourselves and believed yourselves to be evil. You carried on and worshipped all kinds of things, and in your fear of displeasing God you began to sacrifice humans to God. You carried so much fear of what you did that you began to ask for rules. You prayed to God, actually you prayed to several Gods, and you asked to be saved from your own sins. You did not wish to be forgiven yet. You only asked to be saved. This was long before you became aware that you needed help. You believed that you would do well with rules - a good set of rules will straighten everything right out. So today you create governments and ask them to make your rules - habit, it's all habit. So now it's time to give up this habit of living by rules. Just be who you are. No rules and no punishment for breaking your own rules. Let's believe in "live and let live" and allow everyone to grow at their own pace

No one will harm you if *you* do not allow them to. You draw what you are. Change you and you will change what you draw. Rules are not necessary and you will wish to know that in your future your governments will not be making laws for you to follow nor will they be enforcing these laws. In your future your government will learn to direct each nation into educational and electrical and medical studies. Most of your funds will go to education of the whole and your energies will be guided to "see" this universe, not through technology but through your own intuitive powers.

Great healing facilities will be teaching individuals to heal themselves, and will not be cutting them up to save them. It is good. Your future is very bright! So don't worry that God cannot pull this off. We have only just begun and we will do wonderful things very soon. After all, who would have thought that God would be speaking to you so freely? Everything is possible… absolutely everything.

Once you did not believe that you are indeed God. Now you are uncertain who or what you are. So often you try to create in a manner that is befitting a God. I want you to know that to live your life for you is what is best. Do you not see how you do *all,* as it should be. You do not murder out of lack of knowledge of your Godhood. You murder out of anger and hatred. You do not rape and molest out of not knowing your Godliness. You rape and molest out of your own frustration and fear.

To become God you must *clear.* Clear away the debris that inhabits your own subconscious mind. Allow this debris to leave. It is killing you and maiming you to the extent that you are not functioning as God. Once you clear this blocked energy, you will be capable of loving once again. You do not realize most of your own actions and how they affect you. Once you begin to see how you are being harmed from within, you will wish to go within and clean up your own mess. It's so important to clean your own debris and not worry about the rest of God's cells. If you are working on straightening out the others, it is best to know that you need help most.

Once you let go of straightening out every one else's life, you will be ready to work at cleaning up your own mess. Most of you do not wish to see your own mess as you believe this to be too painful, so you deny that your mess even is. This is how you do this. You read what God writes and you see how this is important for a friend to read, because you know that it refers to that particular friend and is exactly what he or she needs to hear. Well, when you know that the information I write is for a friend, you can be certain that *you* are the one it was written for.

Now, most often you do not wish to hear about you and how you have gone haywire. You don't mind hearing about the rest of the world and how they have messed things up. I want you to know that it is all you. You are the one who made this mess and you are the one who will clean it up. Most often you are not in this because you want to help. Most often you are in this because you want to change and control others. You study and learn metaphysics and spirituality and arm yourself with information and then you go out and begin to fix everyone else first. Stay home and fix you. Do not concern yourself with fixing the rest of the world. It will all fall into place once *you* heal you.

You are the catalyst that will start the healing for this entire body of cells. Don't you see how simple it is? You each have your part to play in this second coming and your part may be as large as healing you. That is the biggest gift you can give to this planet. When you clean out and begin to heal, you are saying "Here, take my body back to God." Do not be afraid to go within and see who you are. Know that you will wish to be well healed in order to experience true love and unconditional support. Most of you are beginning to want more and in the wanting comes the gift. Stay open to receive and all will be yours. You do not wish to be unhappy, you do not wish to be unloved, and you most assuredly do not wish to be alone and separated from God.

You will begin to see all clearly once you clean your windshield. It's tough to drive safely and see clearly with a muddy windshield. No one can clear your windshield but you. Once again I suggest hypnosis and meditation as well as my favorite… enema. Happy clearing!

Once upon a time I sent Christ to earth to teach you how you are God. He did not come to lead you away from your sins so much as to show you your way. Somehow he got caught up in the teaching and leading and it became difficult to be God. You find it difficult to deal with the human side of others and herein lies our problem.

It is easy to feel loving and kind when all is smooth and serene. How do you feel when all is not so serene? I want you to be God at all times, not simply when you are in love or in a peaceful place. So the problem is: how do you act loving when someone is taking away from you or pushing at you? When someone is taking what is yours, you simply say, "I want what is mine," and let it go. When they do not give back what is yours you may ask for intervention on your part. Ask for what you want but do not fight for what you want. Fighting is going into battle and asking for anger and frustration. "Asking for" is being calm and asking.

When you deal with a small child who has taken your jewelry or some other valuable item, you ask him to sweetly to hand it over to you. When he does not, you gently convince him. At no time should you strike this child or anyone else. You do not walk around accusing the child of being a thief because you know that he does not really "see" what he has done. He has not committed a crime in his eyes.

You would do best to look at those who push at you or take from you as this small child. You want what is yours and yet you love and even understand this child. You know that he did not take what is yours out of anger at you. It has nothing to do with you or getting back at you. It is simply his way of playing and having fun. Often on earth you have a "get even" attitude. This is still a game for some of you children.

Do not place too much importance on the child who robs you. Place importance on you. You deserve what you have worked for and you deserve all Gods gifts. One of Gods gifts is love. Give love and you will receive love. Ask to be accepted and you will be. Ask to be loved and you will be. You may ask by doing. Love and love is yours. Accept, and you are accepted. It's that simple. Do not be afraid to go out and retrieve what is yours. Do not do so out of anger or revenge. Do so out of love for you. Be aware that you often judge others who are in your lessons with you and these others are simply your friends who have been asked to help *you* learn. That's all. It's so simple.

All is actually so simple when you begin to get out of the way of God and allow it. You spend a great deal of time not wanting to be God because it is too difficult. Most of you believe that you must smile all day and think peace and love. Be yourself. Be who you are and do it *with* love. It's okay to ask for what you want and it's okay to get what you want. How you ask and how you get is what you must "get out of the way" of. Do not get involved. You let your emotions rule you and you become upset and angry and your hair falls out and you get wrinkles. Stop punishing yourself and go with the flow. Accept what has occurred and allow it to move its way to its destination. See where you can straighten it out and then move. Don't be afraid to ask, out of fear that someone will become upset with you. You are not here to be a subject dominated by fear. Often fear controls you and renders you motionless. This is a big problem for your moving ahead in life.

I wish to teach you to move ahead with love and kindness. You have this belief that only fighters survive. This is not so. Only lovers survive. All is not lost, and in our next book titled *The Survival of Love* we will begin our lesson on survival. I will wish to show you how you do not always do or think what is best for you. You most often criticize those who cheat you, and lie to those you fear, or just to those you fear will leave you. Do not lie - because it makes you feel guilty. It is not a commandment or rule. It is simply a better way. You all "feel" so guilty when you lie and cheat. You tell yourself that you do not, but it registers in your self-conscious as guilt. Guilt is self-punishment and denial - punishing yourself for doing wrong and denying that you even did wrong. You accuse you then deny you. You lie then say "it's okay," when some part of you is already judging you for this offense.

We will wish to stop punishing you with guilt because as long as you have guilt you are denying the gifts of this world. I wish to open you to these gifts. It has been most important, in this series of books, to read this information in the order I write it. I do not expect all to do so as you often believe that you know best. However, it is best for your subconscious. I have delivered information in our first four books that has been extreme and there is a purpose. When you are stuck in one way of thinking, I must jar you out of that place. It is not good to move you ahead until you *go back* to where the problem began.

We are ready to move ahead. These first five books are meant to trigger release in your subconscious mind and are very important before moving into your bright prosperous future. You will begin to see a pattern here and you will find your center balance in all this. Do not believe that you are "there" or that you know all the answers. This is why I do not wish you to push this information at others. You are not there yet and you will never get "there." You are here and tomorrow you will be where you are, and the next day you will be where you are. You never arrive because you are God and you constantly and continually move. Begin to move forward. You have been stuck in a rut like a record on a turntable that is stuck and repeats the same line over and over. This record is now being jarred loose so that it may progress into the future. You will do well to listen to and learn by all information in these books.

I do hope you begin to catch on to this simple way of clearing soon. It's so obvious that garbage passes through you and into the colon. Colon cancer is on the rise so let's start where the mess is. It's even logical. You're all so logical; don't you see the logic in this? Open a colon, or x-ray your own, and you will see the problem. So, we have much yet to learn from God's books. Know you and you will begin to see how you are from God.

So far you do not wish to be one of the first to begin this clearing technique out of fear. Some of you fear this clearing and others of you fear ridicule and still others fear "knowing" what and who you are. Not everyone will see immediately. Some will be drawn inward on an emotional level and still others on a physical level. You will see only as much or as little as you have decided to see. You will not rush into past lives unless it is your plan to do so. You will not rush into physical illness unless this is what you are clearing first.

You each have a plan. Your way is no greater nor is it less than another's plan. If you do not begin to see into your future or your past it is due to this plan. You will see what you are willing to see. You will learn as *you* are ready and you will experience all that is necessary for you and your plan. Most of you are with this "A" Team and will be ready for ascension as I promised. Only those whose plan it is to "stay back and prepare and teach" will do so. You are each working at your own rate of vibratory sequence as you move.

Now, the best way to get you to begin to move is by changing you. Change your life. You are stuck in a rut and need to have a little push out of it. Push you. Stop pushing your spouse or your child to grow. Push you to grow. You are the one who needs change and so you constantly push at others to change. Change you and you will see your entire world change. You *are* your world, and simply by changing who you are, you will effectively change the way you view your world. Do not push anyone else into position. This is important. You are being moved and you may effectively move the others by your vibratory level after you have moved. You are not the only one who is moving and in pushing at another, you may push them against their movement or away from their movement.

You don't know the plan so don't mess with the plan. Let it be by letting all be who they are. There is no need to wake up the masses. They are awakening as was meant and they will arrive on your doorstep asking what is going on. When they come, you may answer their questions. When they stop asking, you would do best to stop ordering them to learn. It is not so difficult. Don't preach unless you are asked to. Do not teach unless you are requested and do not lead unless you are invited.

You are all so certain that you know best, and often what you know is simply what is best for you at this particular time in your process. Do not overwhelm the others with information that they are not ready to hear. "Ask and you shall receive" is good enough. Go to your own work and when others are ready they will arrive to help. You are not so certain of your own job so how can you tell the others how to run their lives.

Do not be unkind to those who simply say that you are crazy. You are! You have "lost it" in their minds, and what you have lost is an old belief system. Go about your life and allow others to think what they wish. When you can do this you will be ready to "accept" you, and when you *are* accepting you, they will begin to accept you. It's all you, you know? They don't believe you because you don't trust you enough to accept what you are learning. You feel that you must have "their" approval to make you acceptable and when you learn that your approval is all that is necessary you will begin to move into position *for* acceptance. Once you can accept you, you will begin to let go of them. In letting go of them, you move forward.

Some of you are holding so tightly to others who are not yet ready to move that it becomes difficult for you to move. You wait for acceptance from the others because this is the past programming. You believe it best to be accepted by those you love and this is you not trusting you. When you do trust you, you will find it quite easy to accept you. You do not often see how you create all your own pain and confusion and even rejection. It is okay to "move" out of a relationship if it no longer benefits you to stay. If there are no rewards, why do you hold on to this old way of living? Let go and move into your new way of thinking and believing. Do not try to convince your friends to move with you. You are going on an adventure and you wish to take all who will listen. Go alone! You have found the way and it is simply your way.

Stay if you must and wait for the others you share with, but I highly suggest that you move now. The others may never come or they may go in another direction. Do not be afraid to move out and on. It's good to move and learn and grow. What you are saying to the others is what you are most trying to teach you. If you find yourself constantly pushing at them to grow and change, it is you who wishes to grow and change. Don't be afraid. It's not the end, it's just begun.

So far we do not have much interest in sex. I have explained how you give power to sex that is not necessarily that important. In Book Four, I began to shock you with my statements over child molestation and how sex is not wrong. I wish you to know that to have sex is not a bad thing. However, most often you have guilt where sex is concerned. Not all, but the majority of you fear sex. It is too complicated and creates many problems on earth at this time. Sex is not bad and sex is not wrong. Sex is simply something to do. Do it if you wish or don't do it if it doesn't feel good. It's more a game than a job. Somehow you began to twist everything and make a game that was meant for fun into a master plan of some sort. There is no master plan with sex. It's simply moving the energy center within your own body. You created a way in which you might "experience" the motion of energy and it became known as sex.

It was great fun once and now it is feared and judged and condemned and even embraced by some. Stop this nonsense. Sex is simply a feeling of energy movement. Sneezing is an energy movement and you do not restrict it in any way. Stop restricting sex. It is good for you to balance and this is why I chose child molestation as my first sexual topic. You will learn that you *judge* sex to such a great extent that you will not allow you to balance and see this subject differently. The reason sexual crimes are on the rise is because *you* are imprisoning sex. Let go of sex. Let the flow continue. Do not stifle sex, as sex is energy flowing freely.

We of course, wish to choose freely who we play games with and this game of sex is no different. It is simply the way you chose to become man and woman. You decided to become man and woman through energy changes within each form. Each form was charged with spirit energy and its essence. All essence is whole in part and all spirit is part of the whole. When you decided to split your aura or energy field, you chose to direct certain characteristics into each separate form. This was to ensure a good mating, as you wished to create new spirits without splitting you further.

We discussed in Book Two how you first decided to split into female and male essence and this was *your* way of keeping you whole. You were afraid you had lost further power by splitting and so you began to "come together" again with your own self through sex. Sex is good. It allows you to become whole with those you split from. If you could trace your family tree back to the original spirit, you would see that *I am* the original and to have sex with *any* of the spirits is to have sex with God. God is spirit energy and God came here to earth and divided and created as separate beings. Now I am ready to become whole and to come together with *all* of me. Do not stop the sex from flowing. It is simply God's energy flowing in and out and through you.

Sex is not bad or wrong. You just *fear* sex more than you fear death or any other energy on earth. This is your plague that is brought down on you. Fear of sex is creating death. You are dying from sexual guilt and panic. You do not accept sex and sex is energy. You are denying a basic part of you in denying sex. Energy *is* you. Stop shutting off. Stop denying. Accept sex for what it is. Do not override the will of another in any way, or at any time. This is most important. Force is never accepted. Allow all to make their own choices.

Now, for those who read this and simply cannot accept it, I wish you to know that you have great fear of sex and it will help you to choose counseling or therapy as your way *out* of this fear that *you* are holding. Do not judge fear. Remember in our first book, how you are taught that you are the one who created Satan or fear simply by blocking? Stop blocking. Allow all to flow. Be free of guilt and pain by allowing all to exist as it really is. Sex is not a monster. It is a good situation. It is a good experience and it will bring you closer to God.

Now I have given the critics a big bomb to throw. Yes, I am God and I tell you that the energy within you is God force energy. And when you flow with this energy as you do during sex you are becoming "alive" with energy. This energy is me and it is breaking free and moving to flow from you in sexual release. Sexual release is very good for you. You will wish to know that when you release or climax (as you call it) you begin to center. Do not stifle your growth by stifling sex. It is most important. You have stifled sex for thousands of years now and look at how you've done. Not such a good choice I would say. Give a new way a try. You can't lose. You are losing lives from AIDS and sexually transmitted disease, and it is all due to your judgment *against* sex. Stop judging sex in any way, shape, or form. You are cutting off part of you, which is part of God.

You will wish to know that kissing is sex, and touching is sex, and holding hands is sex, and even hugging is sex. Will you stop these next? Some of you have already begun. Many are *afraid* to hold hands in public or be seen kissing in public. Many hide the sex act as well as sexual expressions of love. It's not thought proper, or involuntarily it is blocked. Some of you cannot have sex unless your government gives its approval. How did this get so out of hand? It was never meant to be.

Sex is the single biggest problem facing earth at this time. No - it's not death and destruction - its sex. Sex receives more consternation and cries of woe than any other problem on your planet. Sex is no big deal, so why do you scream so much about sexual abuse? It is not the sex act that is so traumatic. It is the fact that the children absorb the guilt and the pain and the confusion regarding sex from the parent. The child then judges himself or herself as bad, for acting bad. When a child is sexually molested the pain is mostly psychological. There is of course physical pain which heals quickly. The big problem is the guilt he or she carries and tries to unload in a society that won't allow them to.

Why not save the children from guilt of this nature? Begin to "see" sex as it truly is, and they will learn from you that they do not create a big crime for being involved in this act. Most children are so afraid of sex and touching one another that they are growing up to hate and kill one another at a very young age. You teach your children not to trust and not to talk to others, and or course this creates separation and a belief that others are the bad guys. So now your children take drugs to escape, or shoot one another on the streets in gang wars. It's not good to separate yourselves. Enough is enough. Come home to God and be one. Stop the pain and stop the confusion over sex. Give sex a rest. Let it be. Give up this war against sex. It's simply a way of expressing love. Love is God. Allow the children to express their godliness once again.

Please listen, for this is not easy to say to you. You are all so full of fear and judgment toward this subject that this is where I will lose many at this time. Not *to* sex, but through this information regarding sex. I can explain about killing and murder of this planet, and you all bow your heads and think "yes, what a shame," but I speak the truth about this subject and you do not trust that this is me. It is me. I am God and I wish to help those who are ready. Don't give up now. We have come a great distance and you are beginning to balance. Look at your fears. Some of these go back many lifetimes, and in many areas your sexual appetites where suppressed to the extent that women could not, or dared not show her skin above the ankle. Where do these rules of *yours* begin? You have incarnated over and over, and you continue to make rules to restrict who and what you are. You have shut down all your powers and any who retained theirs were hunted as witches.

Hear me now. You are God. Each and every one of you is God, and you are part of everyone else. How can you possibly fear part of your own body? You are God and you no longer act like God because you are so afraid of your own power. Stop fearing power and begin to be who you are... God!

So, now I have upset those who do not wish to accept sex as nothing more than fun. Sex is often traumatic and even paralyzing to those who are forced into it. I wish you to know that it is not sex that paralyzes you; it is your belief that sex is wrong or bad. If you will just change how you view sex, the trauma will leave this area. You create so much guilt over sex that it has been dubbed the "king of guilt." You blame sex for harming you emotionally and even physically. You punish you for having sex and you judge you for not having sex.

You believe sex to be important and yet you hate sex for its power over you. You are giving power over to sex by fearing sex. The physical pain is only due to forcing. Do not force sex and do not judge sex. Allow sex. Allow sex to be enjoyable once again by giving up this belief that it is so important. You have sex out of guilt, or you do sex out of need. Do sex out of joy, out of fun, and out of fulfillment. Not for another, but for you.

Do not fear sex and do not judge sex as a job or a necessity. It is not necessary to make love through sex. You may love without sex. You may also have sex without love. It is no big deal. Don't give it power by putting sex on a throne and making it so special. It feels good and is healthy to release, but it is not the only way to release and it is not the only thing you can do to feel good. Let it be. Allow sex to just be. It's not such a big deal.

Why won't you allow your children to know who they are and how they function? You are teaching them to fear sex and to fear that sex may control them. They believe sex to have this big power over them simply because you warn them about this powerful enemy and tell them how it can destroy their lives. Give sex some time off. Let's put power back in the mind and not in sex drive. Give sex a day off by letting it be just what it is, a simple action that was created by you for your own enjoyment.

You gave it so much thought and concern that you created your own monster. Sex is not the villain. I am not the villain and you are not the villain. No one is at fault. You just didn't know. You thought you were doing wrong because it was so enjoyable to you and of course you are punishing yourselves for your fall from grace, so you do not accept this gift of you. You put rules on how and when and how old you must be. You punish your children for even learning about sex. You have created a big monster out of a gift you once received from your own self. Now you punish you by making sex into a culprit and testing your own power of denial to shut down sex. You are shutting down and denying part of you by shutting off sex. You have created an energy, and in denying this energy you are pushing it way back into you. You are stopping the flow of energy, and this energy was meant to flow through you. *All energy is in motion.* You do not stop energy or you change what is into what is not.

Energy that is buried, or suppressed, or blocked is what we call regressive or negative energy. It is not healthy to hate and you have created hatred of sex. Stop seeing sex as something only meant for those who can overcome it or handle it. It is part of everyone, and meant to be experienced by everyone. No limits and no restrictions.

As in any area of life, there is a balance, and later we will discuss this sex balance and how to achieve it. It is not wrong to touch yourself or love your own body. It never was wrong and it never will be. Enjoy *all* that you have created and love all that you have created. You are learning to move out of your old belief patterns and it is good.

You are very good at what you do and what you do is good. Your only concern is how to do better. Most often you do not see what you do as good. You judge you for mistakes until you have put yourself down to the extent that you begin to *believe* that you are unworthy. Most often you do not know what is or is not good. You are judging you according to what you believe, and what you believe is not always what is. So, how can you put you down for making mistakes when you do not really make mistakes? You fall and I pick you up again. This is no mistake. It is simply me teaching you to be God. If you did not fall, I could not teach you. How can you call falling wrong or bad? You fell from grace and now you judge yourself for this mistake. It is no mistake. It is meant to create further awareness for God.

I stretch my own body to grow. Part of me began to grow and move and leave. That part of me is you. You grew inside of me and then you moved out of God. Now you are beginning to re-enter God. It's not wrong to leave. God does not wish you to judge this any more. You are not meant to stay motionless. You are energy and energy moves. You moved, and the movement created fear. So now you do not wish to move. Movement still creates fear. You do not move out of your homes, or out of jobs you hate, or even out of relationships that are no longer loving. You stay out of fear of what's out there waiting if you choose to claim it.

You fell and you caught yourself and now you are stuck. Un-stick yourself. Remain motion. Do not block movement. Get out of your way by allowing you to be God. God is energy and energy does not remain motionless. It is best to move. Movement is growth. Do not stifle you by stifling motion. Motion is best and motion will return you to God. You drove your car to the beach and saw how good it is and now you do not wish to return. You wish to stay, out of fear that you do not know your own way home. You left and you won't come back and see how you are free to leave again. I love you and I want you to come visit. I am now in the process of painting a road map with arrows, so you may "feel" good about traveling once again.

You see, you are so afraid of falling further from me, that you are clinging to a branch to hold you up. You will not fall *out* of this tree because *you* are this tree. Part of you is afraid to fall out of you, and it is all you in here. There is no falling. It is all you. God is beginning to "realize" how he *created* himself and you. You are one with God and you are one with all that is God.

God is experimenting with time and space and discovering his own body. In this experimentation God has begun to see how he is splitting only he is not really split. He only believes he split because he cannot see how he is 'all.' No other is here in this space. Space is all God and God is in space. No one is here except God. No one can fall and be hurt because there is no bottom to fall to. I am God and I am boundless and I am *in* and around all that is. I go through you and around you and I am you. You are one within God's body and you are functioning out of necessity. Not necessity of life, but out of a necessity to learn to see myself as I truly am.

I believe my body to be in a state of repair and often I send out other me's to tell me how I am doing. I am growing so rapidly in size that I do not know how I will contain myself. Often I send out forces to check on my own progress and tell me who I am. You see, I constantly grow in wisdom and knowledge and energy. I become more of what I am and what I am is me. I must find out who I am through a network of researchers who report back as they investigate what is out there in my own field of energy. One report is that many areas of me have become disoriented and believe they are disconnected or alone. They feel they have fallen out of God and believe they traveled too far in the service of investigation.

You did not go too far. You are still in me. You are my new leaders in this particular area or frontier. You are not lost and all alone. You feel fallen and deserted. You are not. I am right here all around you and I am reminding you of who and what you are. You left so long ago that you belong to someone else now. You changed your energy field and built walls of protection from the outside - only you are not outside. You are still within God's body, only you do not allow God's energy to flow freely within these walls you have built. When you allow this energy to continue into you and out of you, you will remember who you are and how you got here. Then you will no longer fight to stay where you are. You hold on out of fear of falling, and actually there is no where to fall.

You are a baby embryo inside its mother, only you believe you are walking on a cliff. You cannot fall. You can however be born and see the world and life as it really is. No fear is there. You are creating fear. It does not exist. Danger does not exist. You cannot learn to grow by stunting your growth. You cannot learn to expand by allowing yourself no freedom to see. You will find in time that you cannot fall and hurt yourself, as you are *within* you. You are dreaming. Please wake up!

Now that you are beginning to see how you are part of God, it is best to be "one." Love all who are God and allow all to be exactly who and what they are. You do not heal this planet by changing outside influences. You heal this planet by changing you. You are the center of this universe. You are the one who has the power to change energy. You may change energy from fear to love, or you may continue to change it from love to fear. No one is expected to be the sole support system of this planet. You are each responsible for yourself. Not for others, but for you.

You may wish to know that many of your children are incarnating at this time to help you to adjust. Change is good for you and some of what you are seeing in your children is drastically different from what you now accept. The children are your mirror. You will look at them and know where your fears lie. They are good for you. You will find yourselves wanting to judge their behavior. They are showing you what *you* and others have created by your fear. They are not here simply to be your child. They too are part of God and they too are soul energy. And they too may carry big trauma from past life, or just this life. You are not to be so hard with yourself concerning their path. They may have a preordained path and it is not up to you to turn them in another direction.

Now, this is where I will lose some of you. You do not own your children. You do not have the right to direct their lives. They are souls who asked you to permit them to enter earth *through* you. You channeled a soul into being. This does not give you dominion over this soul. You are not their lord and master. You may set rules to follow but you do not *own* them. Allow them to believe and learn and grow. Do not change them into another you. You have not done well in this life and it is best to allow them to find their own way. In pushing the children to do what you believe is best, they are running away from you. You are chasing them out of your family environment and onto the streets of your cities. Begin to *listen* to their needs. Don't suggest that college is the only way, as you went to college. Or maybe you didn't make it, and now you are forcing them to live up to what you did not do - finish your dreams for you. This is not why they are here. They are not here to repeat your mistakes. The children are here to do it differently.

Some of you are so locked-in to old belief patterns, that what was said to be important a few hundred years ago is still on your mind. Let go of some of your axioms as they are incorrect. An apple a day does not keep a doctor away and food is not the problem, thought is. So stop pushing education on your children. What if you are to learn that nothing is more important than to learn to evolve as a soul? Begin to put emphasis where it belongs - on the family unit as a support system for one another. You have changed what was once support and love and understanding into rule and control. You even dictate who shall be friends and who shall not; what your child eats and who your child loves and plays with. If they are not good enough in your eyes, you do not allow your child to grow in a relationship with them.

Who are you to judge? You are sitting in so much debris that you cannot see who you are, or even what is best for you. And you all sit and scream how you know what is best for your child. They are not *your* child. They are *my* child and I am asking you to back off and let them grow. Inherent right is not right. Do not love only when they are good. Love and *accept* them when they do wrong (in your eyes), and love and support them in their choices. You believe that because you spend your money on them, and clothe them, and were there when they could not feed themselves or change their own diapers, that you now have eternal right to this body. You do not own this soul. It is not yours. You may not beat it or punish it physically. One soul was never meant to harm another soul in any way. You shout physical abuse if someone (an adult) should slap you or hit you. Look at what you are doing. Just because you gave birth does not give you free rein to punish or abuse. Physical violence is not acceptable in my "A" Team.

Now, I do not wish you to judge you for your past. The past is done and we are moving into enlightenment. It is not so easy to look at our own reflection at times. When you look around your world you will "see" who you are and how you have created in your life. The violence of this planet is a direct reflection of your buried physical need for violence. This need comes from anger at the self for past deeds. It is buried and must surface. Look at who you are. How many lives have you lived? How often did you murder or create what you believed to be crimes? You carry this guilt and more. Your subconscious is full to overflowing and your anger at who you were, and are, is spilling over into the streets of this planet.

You are not who you believe. Please begin to forgive you. You are judging you for past sins and I am trying to convince you that there are no sins. You are so set on punishment that you will not believe me when I tell you that there is *no wrong*, not ever. You do not create out of love of you. You wish to punish you for being bad, so you punish anyone who does not see as you do. You stop them from being who they are because *you* are so afraid of more pain. You are the one inflicting pain on yourself. Stop this and stop it now. You can begin to let you be by letting others be. It's not so difficult to get back on track. Let go of this need to punish. It is reflecting back at you now from your streets.

Self punishment is very big on earth, and your need to punish you shows in your penance for sins. You tell a priest or rabbi your problem areas and they tell you how to overcome your evil ways by penance or labor or chastity. Do not continue this form of punishment. It is simply a symbol of a much larger problem. Let go of penance and guilt inflicted by judgment. Do not walk around with the knowledge that you live a good life because you believe you have never done "bad." You, who have restricted yourselves to live within the rules, carry most of your guilt with you. You do not release and you are ready to explode from holding everything in. Get it out. Put your cards on the table. Scream and shout and say what is really bothering you.

Do not use physical violence when you release. Psychotherapy is best as it allows you to release in degrees. You did not arrive where you are overnight and you will not return overnight. Do not punish you and do not punish your child. Give them time to think and be who they are. Talk and listen. Mostly - *you* order. You do not listen well at all. I wish you to begin to "see" through their eyes. Stop judging them and they will begin to feel loved again. The children are in a great deal of pain. They are not accepted and are judged at every turn. Yes, I know they are dangerous with their guns and knives and restricted emotions, but they are *your* reflection. Do you see how dangerous you have become to yourself? Give love and understanding a try. Stick by them. Listen to them. *Know* them. You created this situation for you to grow by. Do what you planned. Don't change the children, change you and watch your children grow up in love instead of fear.

※

Once upon a time I created heaven and earth. Heaven is all that is and earth is only a small part of what is. This is not to say that earth is not important. She is quite important in the scheme of things. She is the one place where I can learn to balance. Long ago I began to clarify for myself exactly who or what I am. I began to create confusion by not knowing how I existed or where I existed. I began to see me as something unknown to me. I started to eliminate parts of myself and concentrate on what this felt like. After eliminating myself in certain areas I would, and could, easily reclaim these parts. This is similar to a small baby who investigates his fingers and toes. Once I discovered a new part of me, I would push, or shove, or just look at it until it moved, or did something to show me its true meaning. I was certain that each and every part of me had a function.

Much in the same way that you on earth dissect and study human bodies (usually corpses), I began to dissect and study my body. I wanted to know all there was to know about how I got here. So here I am, investigating myself and pushing at parts within me that moved, and shoving at parts that did not, simply to see if they would eventually move. And I come across a part of me who does not move. It is frozen in time. It forgot to evolve. It is stuck in its own turmoil and it is now being "pushed" to move. Guess who this part is? Yes... you on earth.

So, begin to move or I will continue to push at you. Your lives are not meant to be stagnant. You are meant to be aware of your place within God. God is pushing at you to wake you up. In the same way that you nudge a sleeping body to wake him or her. I am waking you up and you will like this new day that is dawning. You have slumbered and dreamt for a long time and you are still "in" your dream. Wake up! This is not real, it is a dream. I will show you what *is* real.

Now I wish to thank you for reading our fifth book and ask you to please continue reading my books. I will guide this girl who writes for me to write several more books, and she will continue to write for me. You will not be let down by her, and I will not quit until I see the sleep leave your eyes. I want you all "clear" eyed and wide awake for our second coming. For now I will bid you a fond aloha. Liane will be ready to begin our sixth book very soon. Good day and God bless you *real* good!

God

~ *Epilogue* ~

Once upon a time I came to earth to teach how to love. God does not wish to intervene nor to appear in human form. I am not human and this would only confuse the masses. So here I sit, writing quietly *through* human form. The only way to get you to wake up is to nudge you. I do not wish to shock you, so I will not pounce on you. I will gently whisper to you and slightly move you until you are awake. To appear out of the sky, or even to appear on a street corner and begin to move tall buildings and make things disappear would only create chaos. Some would fall in their knees in response and I would never get them up.

You are so accustom to "following" that you will no longer listen to you, however you would listen to this great God who appeared from nowhere to prove to you how he is God. I do not want you to follow me. I want you to follow you. You are God and you must learn to accept that you are your own source. Do not give up being God. Do not give your power back to me or to any other spirit. *You are God.* Act like it, know it and be it.

Do not wait for the rest to catch on out of fear of being lonely. It is not so lonely as you believe. Once you climb to a level of awareness and acceptance that is best for you, you will draw others who are ready to learn and accept. The key word here is acceptance. *You* must accept what you believe, and when you begin to really accept you as God, others will believe and you will no longer be alone. Do not deny who you are. Do not judge anyone or anything. When you no longer judge others you will no longer draw those who judge you.

I will now end with this promise. I will never stop loving you… you are me and I am you!

God's Pen

I first heard the voice of God in 1988. I was sitting in my back yard reading a book when this big booming voice interrupted with, "I am God and I will not come to you by any other name." I felt like the voice was everywhere - inside of me as well as in the sky around me. I was so frightened that I ran in my bedroom to hide.

This was not the first time that I heard voices. I had been communicating with my own spirit guide or soul for about a year. I guess my depth of fear regarding God, and all that he represented to me at the time, was just too much.

I spent two days trying to avoid the voice of God, which was patiently waiting for me to respond. By the second day I was exhausted from lack of sleep and decided to give in and talk with him. This turned out to be the greatest gift and best decision of my life.

This first book shows my evolution from communicating with my soul to communicating with the Big Guy. It took a couple years for me to be comfortable communicating with God. My fear of a punishing God was big! That has most definitely changed and I now think of God as my partner and best friend.

In the beginning the voice of God would wake me in the middle of the night and tell me it was time to write. He said I had promised to do this work (I assumed he was talking about the soul/spirit me). I would drag myself up to a sitting position and watch in amazement as my hand flew across the page, while I tried to keep up by reading what was being written.

It was always so much fun to wake up the next morning and grab my notebook to see what God had written during the night. After some time the voice stopped waking me and I became comfortable picking up my pen and writing for God first thing in the morning. I think in the beginning I had to be awakened while still semi-conscious from sleep so I wouldn't object too much to the information that was being channeled through me.

As I grew less and less afraid (and more trusting) of God, he was able to communicate greater information. Some of the information is quit controversial, but I felt it important to just let it be and not censor it. I present the writings here to you as they were given to me. I have edited a little (mostly the more personal information regarding myself) and I have used a pen name for privacy reasons. I asked God for a good pen name and he guided me to Liane which (I was told) in Hebrew means "God has answered."

At one point I became a little concerned about my sanity in all this, so I went to a hypnotherapist to find out what I was doing. Under hypnosis I saw this incredibly huge beam of light with a voice coming from within it. It was a giant "loving light" and felt so comforting and kind. It felt like that's where I came from. After that I stopped worrying about my sanity. If this is crazy, I think it's a very good kind of crazy to be....

In loving light, Liane

Loving Light Books
www.lovinglightbooks.com

Made in the USA
Lexington, KY
10 February 2010